PARA/INQUIRY

S0-AIS-595

"For those of us who live in virtual cultures, Victor Taylor articulates a new way of reverence, the 'parasacred'. Taylor's religious task is postmodernity's spiritual quest: to get beyond sacred–profane dichotomies into something both more contemporary and more authentic."
        Tom Beaudoin, author of *Virtual Faith: The Irreverent Spiritual Quest of Generation X*

In *Para/Inquiry: Postmodern Religion and Culture*, Victor E. Taylor brings into conversation a wide range of critical perspectives, emphasizing the interdisciplinary character of postmodern thought through the writings of Jean-François Lyotard and other contemporary and past philosophers, artists, and writers. Taylor writes in a postmodern prose style, combining textual analysis and intellectual experimentation that, we see, calls for a re-envisioning of the postmodern condition.

Central to the book is the status of the sacred in postmodern times. Taylor explores the transfiguration of sacred images in art, culture, and literature. What develops is a concept of the sacred that is singular and resistant to an easy assimilation into artistic, cultural, or narrative forms. With chapters on psychoanalysis and literature, Holocaust studies, religion, art, and postmodern culture, Taylor argues for an extending of the postmodern condition that insistently requires us to engage anew the topics of knowledge, creativity, ethics, and politics.

Anyone wishing to gain a fresh approach to postmodernism will find this book a joy to read.

Victor E. Taylor teaches in the Department of English and Humanities at York College of Pennsylvania. He is co-editor of *Postmodernism: Critical Concepts* (Routledge 1998) and the *Routledge Encyclopedia of Postmodernism: Disciplines, Terms and Figures* (Routledge forthcoming). He is also the editor of the on-line *Journal for Cultural and Religious Theory* (www. jcrt.org).

CABRINI COLLEGE LIBRARY
610 KING OF PRUSSIA ROAD
RADNOR, PA 19087

PARA/ INQUIRY

Postmodern Religion and Culture

Victor E. Taylor

CABRINI COLLEGE LIBRARY
610 KING OF PRUSSIA ROAD
RADNOR, PA 19087

London and New York

#40990130

First published 2000
by Routledge
11 New Fetter Lane, London EC4P 4EE

Simultaneously published in the USA and Canada
by Routledge
29 West 35th Street, New York, NY 10001

Routledge is an imprint of the Taylor & Francis Group

© 2000 Victor E. Taylor

Typeset in Grotesque and Galliard by Routledge
Printed and bound in Great Britain by
TJ International Ltd, Padstow, Cornwall

All rights reserved. No part of this book may be
reprinted or reproduced or utilized in any form or by
any electronic, mechanical, or other means, now
known or hereafter invented, including photocopying
and recording, or in any information storage or
retrieval system, without permission in
writing from the publishers.

British Library Cataloguing in Publication Data
A catalogue record for this book is available from the
British Library

Library of Congress Cataloging-in-Publication Data
Taylor, Victor E.
          Para/Inquiry: postmodern religion and
          culture / Victor. E. Taylor.
          p. cm.
          Includes bibliographical references and index.
1. Postmodernism—Religious aspects.   I. Title.
BL65.P73T38 1999   99-20816
149'.97—dc21 CIP

ISBN 0–415–18902–0 (hbk)
ISBN 0–415–18903–9 (pbk)

FOR SUSAN

CONTENTS

FIGURES

ACKNOWLEDGMENTS

I am deeply indebted to Charles E. Winquist, Charles H. Long, James Wiggins, Mark C. Taylor, and Bill Readings (1960–94) for their thoughtful commentary at various stages of this endeavor. I also owe debts of gratitude to the National Endowment for the Humanities/DAAD and the School of Criticism and Theory at Cornell University. York College of Pennsylvania, with the much appreciated support of my department chair, Dr Edward Trostle Jones, generously granted me release time to finish the final editing of the manuscript. Finally, I am enormously fortunate and grateful to have had the support and expertise of my very capable editors at Routledge, Adrian Driscoll and Tony Bruce, and editorial assistant, Anna Gerber, and production editor, Sarah Hall.

The extract from T.S. Eliot's *Selected Essays* ('Religion and Literature') is quoted with the kind permission of Faber & Faber Ltd.

Posting

Finally, there is no existence that is constant, either of our being or of that of objects. And we, and our judgment, and all mortal things go on flowing and rolling unceasingly. Thus nothing certain can be established about one thing by another, both the judging and the judged being in continual change and motion.

(Michel de Montaigne, *Apology for Raymond Sebond*)[1]

The time for me hasn't come yet; some are born posthumously.[2]

(Friedrich Nietzsche, *Ecce Homo*)

If there are margins, is there still *a* philosophy, *the* philosophy?

(Jacques Derrida, *The Margins of Philosophy*)[3]

BEFORE THE POST

(A) ... addressing the semantic complexity of postmodernism. Is it an intellectual movement? Is it an historical event? Indulging in such questioning resists Montaigne's assertion that existence, whether of beings or objects or concepts, is caught in a continuous process of change and motion. Defining postmodernism as a concept or a movement, or fastening it to the seemingly uninterrupted timeline of the Western philosophical tradition, presupposes that postmodernism *is* something or that it is something that *has happened* or that it is something *happening* or that it is *born* in its own time.[4]

Between words and objects one can create new relations and specify characteristics of language and objects generally ignored in everyday life.

(René Magritte, letter to Foucault)[5]

(B) Friedrich Nietzsche, the estranged father of postmodernism, speculated that his radical philosophy would be born posthumously. One may ask if Nietzsche's dream of an ideal radicality now has found its realization in postmodernism. One could well argue that any radical philosophy, even Nietzsche's oppositional binarism and recurring dream of aesthetic unity, is shaped, if not determined, by the insistent structurality of philosophy. Is it the case that postmodernism's turn toward the discursive margin radicalizes the Western philosophical structure? In holding, however tenuously, to the belief that postmodernism is a radical turn, one is in effect claiming that postmodernism begins with its own disinheritance from philosophy and the very metaphysics of meaning that have directed philosophical inquiry since Plato. What, then, is one to make of this relationship between postmodernism's supposed radicality and its metaphysical (dis)inheritance?

(C) Jacques Derrida, Nietzsche's heir-apparent, in a seminal text entitled "Structure, Sign, and Play in the Discourse of the Human Sciences," writes that "in the absence of a center or origin, everything became discourse ... that is to say, a system in which the central signified, the original or transcendental signified, is never absolutely present outside a system of differences."[6] As a result, "[t]he absence of the transcendental signified extends the domain and the play of signification infinitely."[7] This displacement of the transcendental signified, I will offer, becomes the "founding" instance of linguistic disinheritance that is generally understood as the postmodern (see Glossary). Linguistic disinheritance is an event in which philosophical and literary meaning are cut off from absolute presence, absolute center. Derrida more fully elaborates the turn from this tradition of the metaphysics of meaning that founds philosophical inquiry alongside its line of modernist "destroyers":

> Nietzsche, Freud, and Heidegger, for example, worked within the inherited concepts of metaphysics. Since these concepts are not elements or atoms, and since they are taken from a syntax and a system, every particular borrowing brings along with it the whole of metaphysics. This is what allows these destroyers to destroy each other reciprocally – for example, Heidegger regarding Nietzsche, with as much lucidity and rigor as bad faith and misconstruction, as the last metaphysician, the last "Platonist." One could do the same for Heidegger himself, for Freud, or for a number of others. And today no exercise is more widespread.[8]

(D)   If Derrida's "Structure, Sign, and Play" inaugurates a metacritque of the Western philosophical tradition *à la* Nietzsche, as this passage suggests, it can be said that the overall force of Continental philosophy since the late 1960s and early 1970s has been to define philosophical concepts as singular elements that, while taken from a syntax and a system, do not subsequently borrow the whole of metaphysics from Western philosophical thought. Poststructuralism and, more generally, postmodernism, in this regard, have an aversion toward, or attempt to more completely destroy, totalized totality and mere opposition.[9]

(E)   Postmodernism, as it is disinherited from the totality–opposition schema of the modernist destroyers, expresses an in-betweenness or an alongsideness of the tradition.[10] It is around these two spatial metaphors that I discuss postmodernism and elaborate it as (para) inquiry. Postmodernism, then, may be found(ed) in between or alongside

4

philosophy and literature, cultural texts and history, death and the sacred.

AFTER THE POST

(F)   The *post*modern age rests partially covered by the late modern. The *post*-prefix of postmodernism has several possible connotations. First, *post*modernism is after modernism; second, *post*modernism is against modernism; third, *post*modernism is a continuation of (high) modernism. The difficulty with defining the *post*- prefix comes from its positioning within the temporal order.[11] The *post* suggests some*thing* some*where* in history. Postmodernism often is placed under the umbrella of postmodernity. This, however, is not sufficient in so far as postmodernity marks an historical era, and is most widely used as a sociological term referring to the social order under late capitalism.[12] Postmodernism, I argue, is more than an annoying symptom of a post-industrial–late-capitalist social organization. In fact, postmodernism is more than temporality, and more than history and the process of history. In a sense, we must return to Montaigne's postulate and once again see the difficulty in establishing a set of relations, a set of measurements, and a cataloging system that reduces one thing to another. The difficulty in defining postmodernism lies in establishing a center out of which flows a coherence.[13] Coherence, totality, oppositionality, and systematicity begin with a center, an original point that is, in effect, a gathering together of meaning which pre-empts all prefixes.

> Where and how does this decentering, this thinking the structurality of structure, occur?
> (Jacques Derrida, *Writing and Difference*)

(G)   Postmodernism is not contained within a continuum of subtle arguments and propositions.[14] For instance, unlike the "paradigmatic shifts" one finds across the ages – for example, the Copernican revolution in which the centrality of earth gives way to the centrality of the sun, with centrality continuing as a concept – postmodernism "shifts" the continuum altogether. In other words, the conceptual structurality of the universe did not change when the sun displaced the earth, assuming its centrality. In postmodernism, however, the conceptual structurality of the universe has changed in the sense that the items within the frame shift in relation to the displacement of the frame. In postmodernism, the totality of the universe and the continuity of frame gives way to the discontinuous frame and the radical heterogeneity of the universe.

ALONGSIDE THE POST

(H)   It is in the alleged continuum of philosophical thought across the ages that postmodernism may be incorrectly read as the most recent instalment in a series of perspectives. This is not to say that postmodernism is not part of the Western philosophical conversation. It is, in fact, an extremely significant part; but it does not stand entirely within the frame of the Western philosophical tradition. Postmodernism is not, I hasten to add, without a frame. Indeed, postmodernism has a multiplicity of frames and framings. Postmodernism occurs around the frame of philosophy to the extent that a frame leaves something outside of itself and that which is outside is often left unnoticed (Derrida's margins of philosophy). Para/inquiry, then, is that which is left outside or around the center. Thinking as para/inquiry shows that centrality is impossible to the extent that one must simultaneously include and exclude an outside, a para. *Para/Inquiry: Postmodern Religion and Culture* is concerned with the margins of inquiry; it is concerned with inquiry before it finds its rule – its inside and its outside – its frame.

CHAPTER 1

Paralogies

To refute the prejudice anchored in the reader by centuries of humanism and of "human sciences" that there is "man," that there is "language," that the former makes use of the latter for his own ends, and that if he does not succeed in attaining these ends, it is for want of good control over language "by means" of a "better" language [*c'est faute d'un bon contrôle sur le langage 'au moyen d'un 'meilleur langage*].

(Jean-François Lyotard, *The Differend*)

For reading a text is never a scholarly exercise in search of what is signified, still less a highly textual exercise in search of a signifier. Rather, it is a productive use of the literary machine, a montage of desiring machines, a schizoid exercise that extracts from the text its revolutionary force [*exercise schizoïde qui dégage du texte sa puissance révolutionnaire*]. The exclamation "So it's … !", or the meditation of *Igitur* on race, in an essential relationship with madness.

(Deleuze and Guattari, *Anti-Œdipus*)

I arrive, now, at the ineffable center of my story. And here begins my despair as a writer. All language is an alphabet of symbols whose use presupposes a past shared by all the other interlocutors. How, then, transmit to others the infinite Aleph, which my fearful mind [*temerosa memoria*] scarcely encompasses? The mystics, in similar situations, are lavish with emblems: to signify the divinity, a Persian speaks of a bird that in some way is all birds; Alanus de Insulis speaks of a sphere whose center is everywhere and whose circumference is nowhere; Ezekiel, of an angel with four faces who

9

looks simultaneously to the Orient and the Occident, to the North and the South. (Not vainly do I recall these inconceivable analogies; they bear some relation to the Aleph.) Perhaps the gods would not be against my finding an equivalent image, but then this report would be contaminated with literature, with falsehood. For the rest, the central problem is unsolvable: the enumeration even if only partial, of an infinite complex [*la enumeracíon, siquiera parcial, de un conjunto infinito*].

(Jorge Luis Borges, "The Aleph," *Labyrinths*)

Whenever a butterfly appears my gaze is first directed to it as to a being newly created that very moment, and secondly the words "butterfly – has been recorded" are spoken into my nerves by the voices; this shows that one thought I could possibly no longer recognize a butterfly and therefore examines me to find out whether I still know the meaning of the word "butterfly."

(Daniel Paul Schreber, *Memoirs of My Nervous Illness*)

What would it mean to adequately disclose the relationship between language and the world? For Jean-François Lyotard, this would-be disclosure is preceded by a dramatic foreclosure on "… the metaphysical doctrines of modern times."[1] Like other postmodernists, Lyotard believes that language does not reveal the meaning of the world, nor does the world reveal the meaning of language. We, as subjects of postmodernism, nevertheless, desire (fear the lack of) this *finalité*, and it is this impossible condition of transmitting the "infinite Aleph" of Borges that necessitates turning to the "contaminate" of literature to reconcile, much like Daniel Paul Schreber, our minds to the world.

Lyotard's *enjeu*, Deleuze and Guattari's *machines désirantes*, Borges's *conjunto infinito*, and Schreber's "butterfly" all point toward a failure of intelligibility within the age of postmodernism. There is a profound lack of, and an equally profound desire for, meaning and value within language and life in the age of postmodernism. Perhaps it is Deleuze and Guattari's Doctor Schreber who best represents the postmodern relationship to the concept of intelligibility. Culture, literature, philosophy, and theology together form organs of expression, with each contributing to the attempted triumph over the unintelligible. Each word, each sentence, each chapter of Schreber's *Memoirs of My Nervous Illness* is an overflowing of an organ. Not only must we, Schreber's postmodern descendants, form a relationship with the unintelligible by way of his madness; we must become mad by listening to the ways in which his words misfit with our narrative of reality. We, then, must also attend to the silences of his desire for meaning and value that punctuate the innumerable small abysses forming between language and world. After Schreber's madness and, perhaps, our own, the work of philosophy is no longer disciplinarily bound to intelligibility, but instead becomes loosened, paralogical and experimental; postmodern inquiry, free from Enlightenment lucidity, is a form a madness born from the unintelligible coupling of language and world; para/inquiry, as a postmodern philosophy, must forfeit the syllogism to the ambiguous non-totality of spoken and unspoken phrases of desire that comprise the universe. Inquiry must contract a nervous illness.

10

THE BOOK IS OPEN

> When we relate desire to Oedipus, we are condemned to ignore the productive nature of desire: we condemn desire to vague dreams or imaginations that are merely conscious expressions of it; we relate it to independent existences – the father, the mother, the begetters. ... The question of the father is like that of God: born of abstraction [*née de l'abstraction*], it assumes a link to be already broken between man and nature, man and world, so that man must be produced as man by something exterior to nature and to man. On this point Nietzsche makes a remark completely akin to those of Marx and Engels: "We now laugh when we find 'Man' *and* 'World' placed beside one another, separated by the sublime presumption of the little word 'and'."
>
> (Deleuze and Guattari, *Anti-Œdipus*)

Within his own writings, which have become emblematic of a schizophrenic mind, perhaps the most famous and most studied schizophrenic mind in the history of psychiatry, Daniel Paul Schreber displayed the ability to read his own symptomology and see himself as man *and* God, father *and* mother, man *and* woman. It is these schizophrenic delusions, coupled with a certain clarity of interpretation, that point to more than the simple conclusion that Schreber was adept at viewing his own madness or able to understand his own visions as minor departures from objective reality. Schreber's multiple visions of himself call into question the very reality of objectivity for us all. His madness, measured by his latent rationality, enabled him to fold his symptoms back onto his psyche, crafting them into language:

> All this naturally only in my imagination [*Vorstellung*], but in a manner that the rays get the impression that these objects and phenomena really exist. I can also picture myself in a different place, for instance while playing the piano I see myself at the same time standing in front of a mirror in the adjoining room in female attire; when I am lying in bed at night I can give myself and the rays the impression that my body has female breasts and a female sexual organ.[2]

Daniel Paul Schreber's psychopathology cannot be dismissed as a generic "loss of mind." Instead, it should be considered a loosening of mind. His "mind," to the reader, is all too present in his memoirs, and it is this presence of mind that draws the attention of psychiatry, which may ask if Schreber's self-reflection is indeed all that different from the normalizing or objectifying practices of forming the world into language: Is it the world that governs the reality of language or language that governs the reality of the world? For Schreber, it seems, the latter is the case. His memoirs direct language to encompass the world and shape reality. This ability to control language and form the world by properly distinguishing between "appearing as" and "being" man, woman, or God allows Schreber a small interstitial space within rationality. If we were to view Schreber's delusions not as a psychiatric condition but as philosophical/epistemological problems concerning the relationship between the world and language, we would see, I will argue, the eruption of an aporia that permanently separates the perceived and the real. In the end, we also may find that, Nietzsche's laughter – terrifying as it is – at the "little word 'and'" is an echo of our own.

11

PARAREALITIES

> Having lived for months among miracles, I was inclined to take more or less everything I saw for a miracle. Accordingly I did not know whether to take the streets of Leipzig through which I traveled as only theater props, perhaps in the fashion in which Prince Potemkin is said to have put them up for Empress Catherine II of Russia during her travels through the desolate country, so as to give her the impression of a flourishing countryside. At Dresden Station, it is true, I saw a fair number of people who gave the impression of being railway passengers.
>
> (Daniel Paul Schreber, *Memoirs of My Nervous Illness*)

> We do not write with our neuroses. Neuroses or psychoses are not passages of life, but states into which we fall when the process is interrupted, blocked, or plugged up. Illness is not a process but a stopping of the process, as in "the Nietzsche case." Moreover, the writer as such is not a patient but rather a physician, the physician of himself and of the world.
>
> (Gilles Deleuze, *Essays Critical and Clinical*)

From a literary critic's perspective, it is easy to see the significance of a "reality" suspended between psychosis and language. Following this tension, one can read Schreber's text as either a medical document or a literary creation. To do either, however, necessitates working through the relationship between language and the world.

In his book *Pararealities: The Nature of Our Fictions and How We Know Them*, Floyd Merrell defines fiction as a complex psychological, linguistic, and social negotiation between a perceived world and a real world:

(a) A fiction is an imaginary construct. It is the re-collection of a set of objects, acts, or events into an alternative "world" which is in some way a *semblance* of (part of) the/a "real world."

(b) A fiction is a *model* in so far as, portraying a "world," it is necessarily a *selective abstraction* from (part of) the/a "real world."

(c) Fictions include: at the lower level of organizational complexity, all figurative uses of language (metaphors, puns, jokes, lies, stories, etc.), and at the upper level, myths, folktales, artistic constructs, historical and philosophical constructs, scientific models, mathematical systems, etc.

(d) A fiction is (usually but not always) conveyed by means of a *language* (written, spoken or non-verbal). The notion of a language as a medium for constructing fictions is limited – in its inquiry – to *natural* and *artificial* (mathematical, logical, etc.) *languages.*

(e) These languages are characterized as *arbitrary*; that is, in the beginning there is no necessary relationship between word and object.[3]

The structurality of the structure of literature, like the structurality of the structure of the Western philosophical tradition, makes explicit the important relationship between the realm of language and the realm of objects and acts. Merrell's emphasis on the parareality of fiction leads to the important question concerning the metaphysics of texts: Are texts samplings of the/a real world? Current literary studies or literary criticism posit that literature is indeed a reflection of the times in which it is written. Analyzing texts comes to be an exegitical

procedure culminating in the identification of the socio-historical indicators that are characteristic of any given era. Representational theories of race, gender, class, and sexuality, as they are applied to texts as themes, ignore the parareality present in the structurality of the structure of literature; these positivistic approaches to texts, collected under the guise of literary exegesis, serve to maintain a naïve isomorphic relationship between language and world. Merrell's point of contention, a point widely shared among postmodern scholars, is that such a simplistic and, perhaps, uncritical linkage of language to world leaves out the process of semiosis that motivates language's becoming fiction, and Schreber's madness becoming philosophy.

It is not so much that literature itself has changed, evolving mechanisms to resist criticism, as it is the continual changing of the world itself. Literature traditionally has been viewed as uniquely *dynamic*, and the world that it mimics as predictably *static*. Merrell's point, as others too have argued, is that *both* are dynamic. Not only do culture and history alter their delicate pose for the writer and reader, but the nature of human knowing shifts as well. There is, within the postmodern, no pre-linguistic world that becomes subject to a cognitive régime of phrasing. The age of criticism as literary "snapshot" has passed away and we must now, as Merrell points out, contend with the unpredictability of intertextuality and the play of ambiguity

since traditional lines of demarcation between disciplines are rapidly converging: physics with chemistry and biology, biology with psychology, psychology with linguistics, history and philosophy with critical theory, and so on. This is not a mere coincidence. A revised world perspective, slowly emerging since the latter part of the nineteenth century, has been catalyzed by relativity and quantum theory, modern and postmodern art, theory and criticism, and departures from conventional metaphysics.[4]

This emphasis on intertextuality and the ambiguity of language aids in clarifying the epigraphs from Deleuze and Guattari, and Borges. Reading (or writing) a text is not merely a cognitive act, nor is it simply exegetical; it is a multi-textual activity or a schizoid exercise that extracts from the text its "revolutionary force." Where Deleuze and Guattari see the persistence of the heterogrammatical structurality of language as revolutionary, their critics see a ludic enterprise. A schizoid exercise is ludic, however, only if one holds an undying belief in lucidity, a one-to-one correspondence between language and world.

Postmodern inquiry, with its intertextual dependency, calls attention to this well-hidden epistemological naïveté of the lucid ideologies that deform semiosis. Within a naïve realism or realist epistemology, language and world unproblematically come together in textuality. Clarity and political/ideological action derive from this metaphysics of materiality, i.e. the/a real world. For Deleuze and Guattari, this is the commonplace scholarly search (applied theory) for the signified that (over)determines the text and yields meaningfulness. For their part, Deleuze and Guattari have complicated the revolutionary character of texts. They offer a revolution of desire as opposed to the widely used sleight-of-hand in which materiality finds itself conjoined with any available political enterprise purporting to be revolutionary.

In *Kafka: Toward a Minor Literature*, Deleuze and Guattari do not view the writer, in this case Franz Kafka, as "a writer-man" [*un homme écrivain*]; instead, Kafka is "a machine-man" [*un homme machine*] and "an experimental-man" [*un homme expérimental*] who falls into language in between the symbolic and the phantasmagoric. In this sense, the revolutionary

13

force of Kafka's text is its becoming, becoming-animal [*devenir-animal*], becoming-inhuman [*devenir-inhuman*]:

> We won't try to find archetypes that would represent Kafka's imaginary, his dynamic, or his bestiary (the archetype works by assimilation, homogenization, and thematics, whereas our method works only where a rupturing and heterogeneous line appears) [*l'archétype procède par assimilation, homogénéisation, thématique, alors que nous ne triuvons notre régle que lorsque se glisse une petite ligne hététrogéne, en rupture*]. Moreover, we aren't looking for any so-called free associations (we are all well aware of the sad fate of these associations that always bring us back to childhood memories [*souvenir d'enfance*] or, even worse, to the phantasm, not because they fail to work but because such a fate is their actual underlying principle). We aren't even trying to interpret, to say that this means that. And we are looking least of all for a structure of formal oppositions and a fully constructed Signifier [*du signifiant tout fait*]; one can always come up with binary oppositions like "bent head–straightened head" or "portrait–sonority" and bi-univocal relations like "bent head–portrait" or "straightened head–sonority." But that is stupid as long as one doesn't see where the system is coming from and going to, how it becomes, and what element is going to play the role of heterogeneity [*le rôle d'hétérogénéité*], a saturating body that makes the whole assembly flow away and that breaks the symbolic structure, no less than it breaks hermeneutic interpretation, the ordinary association of ideas [*l'association d'idées laïque*], and the imaginary archetype.[5]

Deleuze and Guattari's *machine*, minor literature, much like Merrell's new physics, represents a deterritorialization of language. Kafka's K. in *The Trial*, for example, does not receive an acquittal. The horror of the text is not simply that the sentence is carried out; it is the seemingly eternal postponement of the sentence, the Law. One is not asked to choose between guilt or innocence, as if the reader magically were placed in a jury room for deliberation. There is nothing to deliberate, no charge, no evidence, no prosecution or defense. Kafka has, according to Deleuze and Guattari, introduced a minor language, a paragrammar, into the language of the state. Kafka's minor literature moves differently from the major literature of his time. Writing minor literature supplants the dominant structure of the major language by calling attention to the structurality of language, its old physics; in other words, minor literature points out that the dominant has/is a structure. This is the revolutionary force that is extracted from the text.

FOUNDATIONAL FRAGMENTS: INVOKING THE SACRED

> How many styles or genres or literary movements, even very small ones, have only one single dream: to assume a major function in language, to offer themselves as a sort of state language, an official language (for example, psychoanalysis today, which would like to be a master of the signifier, of metaphor, of wordplay). Create the opposite dream: know how to create a becoming-minor. (Is there a hope for philosophy, which for a long time has been an official, referential genre? Let us profit from this moment in which antiphilosophy is trying to be a language of power.)
>
> (Deleuze and Guattari, *Kafka*)

14

Writing is an arrogant enumeration of a structure. The revolutionary force of a text brings forward the limitlessness of written language and the undecideability of interpretation. A major literature conceals the variability of language. Not only is a major language dominant, it is indeed central and sacred. The sacrality of a major literature is not merely expressed stylistically. Its sacrality affirms its centrality. Kafka, the writer, stood outside of the German literary tradition; Kafka, the Jew, stood outside of German culture. In one respect, the Czech and Yiddish speaker caught within the German language finds a resonance with the Jews suspended in the Diaspora. Language and religion are bound to national and linguistic identity, and it is the sacrality of both structures that fashions a margin for the minor element. Kafka, writing in German, finds that the discursive finite is assembled alongside the imaginative infinite, leading him to uncover an unsolveable problem (the problem of diasporic language) that is much like Borges's inevitable, ineffable center that is everywhere and nowhere: "*La Biblioteca es una esfera cuyo centro cabal es cualquier hexágono, cuya circunferencia es inaccessible.*"[6] [The library is a sphere whose exact center is any one of its hexagons and whose circumference is inaccessible.]

Nevertheless, when writing, one must make an initial cut or have a *topos*, as ill-suited to the infinite as it is. Within a modernist hierarchy, it is the sacred that holds the center firmly in place. Borges's library represents an anti-thesis to this modern hierarchy rather well. The *topos* now in question concerns the presentation of the inaccessible circumference of the circle, here the sacred in the age of postmodernism. The sacred, a well-worn and much abandoned concept today, is generally invoked as that archaic foundation which has been lost or forfeited by collective humanity to a thoroughly (post)modern secular world. The invocation of the sacred, if it is not indeed drowned in an aria of scorn, often includes humanity's recognition of, if not hope for, the possibility of its restoration and, perhaps, redemption after its fall(s) from God and into language. This particular rendering of the sacred is religious and transcendent in place, time, and form.[7] It is the sacred of a religious world, of the modernist poet and artist. It is the sacred for which T.S. Eliot yearns near the end of *The Waste Land*:

> Ganga was sunken, and the limp leaves
> Waited for rain, while the black clouds
> Gathered far distant, over Himavant.
> The jungle crouched, humped in silence.
> Then spoke the thunder
> Da[8]

Without a transcendent sacred, or a transcendent law, or a completed sentence, as in Kafka, one is left asking if there is redemption in literature, as antiphilosophy. Is humanity, in effect, lost, without the redemptive promise of literature (sacrality) in the age of postmodernism? Is there no restoration? No salvation? No fall(s) to reclaim? The sacred in the age of postmodernism includes all that modernism recognized, with an important difference: The sacred, with its archaic foundation, its promise, its secret, cannot be restored to its former grandeur; it must be substituted for, and that substitution is always non-transcendent, inadequate, infinite, and necessary. The question that remains is: How does one account for this emergence of a radical difference within the sacred? This question brings us to postmodernism.

15

ARRIVING AT THE POSTMODERN CENTERS

Immanuel Kant's *Aufklärung* merely anticipates the uniformity of Enlightenment, just as the age of postmodernism anticipates the heterogeneity of the postmodern: "If we are asked, 'Do we now live in an enlightened age?' the answer is, 'No, but we do live in the age of enlightenment.'"[9] In other words, a postmodern sensibility, like Enlightenment in Kant's time, has yet to arrive. Defining postmodernism is similar to wandering Borges's labyrinthine library. One can argue that postmodernism has yet to occur. In this sense, the age of postmodernism is an age of waiting and an age of anxiety. This, in part, is due to the condition of the postmodern; it is an anxious condition because it is not entirely clear why or for what one waits. Jean-François Lyotard introduces the postmodern in *The Postmodern Explained* as paradoxical event in time:

> The postmodern would be that which in the modern invokes the unpresentable in presentation itself, that which refuses the consolation of correct forms, refuses the consensus of taste permitting a common experience of nostalgia for the impossible, and inquires into new presentations – not to take pleasure in them, but to better produce the feeling there is something unpresentable [*mais pour mieux faire sentir qu'il y a de l'imprésentable*]. The postmodern artist or writer is in the position of a philosopher: the text he writes or the work he creates is not in principle governed by preestablished rules and cannot be judged according to a determinant judgment [*d'un jugement déterminant*], by the application of given categories to this text or work. Such rules and categories are what the work and text is investigating. The artist and the

writer therefore work without rules and in order to establish the rules [*règles*] for what *will have been made*. This is why the work and the text can take on the properties of an event; it is also why they would arrive too late for their author, or, in what amounts to the same thing, why the work of making them would always begin too soon. *Post-modern* would be understanding according to the paradox of the future (*post*) anterior (*modo*).[10]

The peculiarity of the age of postmodernism is that one may anxiously await that which has already arrived [*de là aussi qu'ils arrivent trop tard pour leur auteur, ou, ce qui revient au même, que leur mise en oeuvre commence toujours trop tôt*]. And, since it has already arrived, it is yet to arrive. Or, its arrival marks its "not yetness." This paradox, for Lyotard, presents itself in modern art. Modern art was postmodern *before* it was modern. That is to say, modern art was postmodern as long as it did not discover and obey its rules: "Thus understood, postmodernism is not modernism at its end, but in a nascent state, and this state is recurrent"[11] [*Le postmodernisme ainsi entendu n'est pas le modernisme à sa fin, mais à l'état naissant, et cet état est constant*]. If one returns for some clarification to Lyotard's earlier book, *The Postmodern Condition: A Report on Knowledge*, this paradoxical event appears, not as an historical event, but as an event outside of linearity. Lyotard's subtitle is fitting given that he is addressing a crisis in thought; an epistemological and political crisis that is linked to larger or grander narratives of an "age." Again, this is not to say that Lyotard is just reporting on the *state* of knowledge; he is reporting on the *condition* of knowledge.

Simply understood, postmodern is that collection of historical events that take place after modernism. The "post" in this instance merely indicates a conclusion to the modern and the beginning of something afterward and new, postmodernism. This initial and, albeit, literal

16

reading of the "post" depends upon a pre-thought or a condition of thinking which makes possible "history" as a linear progression and procession of happenings, events that can be run together as a continuity from *ontos* to *telos*. This continuity, Borges's enumeration, is not assumed in Lyotard's report on knowledge. For Lyotard, the postmodern comes *before* the modern in the sense that it occurred as a condition and not as an event in a sequence of events. How is this non-linearity possible? The postmodern, for Lyotard, is that instance of instability "prior" to the concretization of rules. It is "before" the event, the writing, the art, is joined to a rule or a grand narrative.

In drawing our attention to the condition of knowledge – that it is conditioned by a larger discursive practice – Lyotard actually postpones the arrival of the postmodern by indicating that, once an event is linked, finds a place beneath the rule, it ceases to be postmodern. The postmodern, then, takes events to be particles within an infinite flux of data. Each event has an undirected trajectory in this flux until it is linked to a grand narrative. The infinite stream of data is cut, and that portion is grafted onto one or many discursive structures. The apportionment, however, is not ontologically determined: "*Enchaîner est nécessaire, un enchaînement ne l'est pas.*"[12] That the event must be linked is not the same as dictating *how* it is to be linked. It is at this point that Lyotard identifies the condition of knowledge as in crisis. Events are likely to be linked to the dominant or grand narratives of the time. These totalizing discourses eclipse the event-particle by totalizing the unstable field of data. These grand narratives attempt to exhaust the infinite stream of data, excluding and delegitimating any and all links that do not fit the direction of the grand narrative itself. Or, as Lyotard has described it, postmodernism is " ... an incredulity toward metanarratives."[13]

Postmodern inquiry, para/inquiry, one could argue from this particular definition, is not the ongoing study of the newest new. Rather, para/inquiry attends to the unstable anterior moment of any specific event in relation to a multiplicity of contexts: "The problem is therefore to determine whether it is possible to have a form of legitimation based solely on paralogy"[14] [*Le Problème est donc de savoir si une légitimation est possible qui s'autoriserait de la seule paralogie*]. This multiplicity of contexts, the world, is inexhaustible; the subject is perpetually exceeded by phrasings and thus remaindered across the ages. What, then, becomes of us without an Archimedean point (subject), lever (method), and world (object)? Because of the possibilities contained within para/inquiry we must think asymptotically. The lines of para-critical thought must never claim an origin, an intersection, nor a destination.

PARADISCOURSES

The "para" of *para/inquiry* is an intervention within the prescriptive "must," "ought to," "rules" of the metanarrative. The prefix "para" qualifies "inquiry" by suspending not only the act of measuring, but the determining quantity of the discourse. *Para-critical* studies defer measurement and determination. Here, it is the "para" that interrupts the allegedly exhaustive act of the critical investigation. The "para" as a prefix also suspends the instantiation of the word itself. *Para-critical* defers criticism, *para-philosophy* defers philosophy, *para-sacrality* defers the sacred, *para-ethics* defers the ethical. "Para" defers the meaning of the word in order that the action never takes language. In this sense, the "para" of *paracritical*, *paraphilosophical*, *parasacrality*, and *paraethics* belongs to the logic of paralogy – beside, aside from, or beyond reason. A paralogism is a faulty syllogism; it "erroneously"

finds difference in sameness or sameness in difference. "Para" is the dangerous prefix which defies the rule of identity, the rule of linkage. "Para" suspends the condensation of the syllogistic rule by first instigating the erring thought and second linking the error to the word or action. The prefix "para" draws attention to the repressed excessiveness of the word – its negative instantiation. The paralogical is a logical necessity, just as the paramedic is a medical necessity. The prefix "para" also indicates a subsidiary state of being or the indeterminacy of the word or action. In many ways, the "para" is a uniquely postmodern "prefix." Like the post, it comes *before* the word to designate the after and, at the same time, it uncovers the darker and more threatening anteriorities of the word brought forth. What follows is a study of the imposition of the "para" in philosophy, literature, and culture. In particular, I examine the dark and threatening anteriorities of the sacred, the human, the ethical, and the grave. In other words, the question which drives this writing is: What was inquiry before it found its rules?

CHAPTER 2

Parastructures of the sacred and literature

What I have to say is largely in support of the following proposition: Literary criticism should be completed by criticism from a definite ethical and theological standpoint. In so far as in any age there is common agreement on ethical and theological matters, so far can literary criticism be substantive. In ages like our own, in which there is no such common agreement, it is the more necessary for Christian readers to scrutinize their reading, especially of works of imagination, with explicit ethical and theological standards.

(T.S. Eliot, "Religion and Literature," *Selected Essays*)

What we found especially reassuring was this: when the sun was right overhead a new group of men came to the shore in an egg from one of the seabirds and dragged an object from the shell. It looked like the tall trunk of a tree, but it had no leaves, only branches at the top. They all toiled together to drag the thing up the hill, which rises from the rocks to far above the dunes and bushes. We watched in awe, for it had long been a sacred place to us, marked untellable years before by one of our wandering tribes with a cairn: one of the innumerable graves of our savior hero, the hunter Heitsi-Eibib, who had died many times, yet never died. What sacrilege were these intruders about to commit? We were trembling in anger and trepidation as we watched the strange men opening up a deep hole among the rocks of our cairn. Into this pit they lowered their bare tree, then carefully steadied it in place with rocks they had removed, adding others to it, raising the mound to the height of a man.

(André Brink, *The Cape of Storms: The First Life of Adamastor*)

21

The fruits of the news of the death of God do away with the flower of His death [*la fleur de mort*] as well as the bud of His life [*le bourgeon de vie*]. For alive or dead, it is still a question of belief: the element of belief has not been abandoned [*on ne sort pas de l'élément de la croyance*]. The announcement of the father's death constitutes a last belief, "a belief by virtue of non-belief" about which Nietzsche says, "This violence always manifests the need for belief, for a prop, for *structure*" Œdipus-as-structure.

(Deleuze and Guattari, *Anti-Œdipus*)

ANTI-STRUCTURE

Postmodern para/inquiry contributes to the reading of the Western literary, philosophical, and theological tradition in so far as it articulates, as Deleuze and Guattari describe it, an (anti)structurality of language that is heterogrammatically revolutionary and founded upon Nietzsche's pronouncement of the death of God. Traditional critical discourses within the humanities, with their concern for an ethical and theological foundation (as evidenced by Eliot's understanding of the relationship between religion and literature), often are directed by the search for an origin, a Nietzschean "prop," that promises to synthesize language and the/a real world. In the age of postmodernism, with its unyielding violence upon linearity, linkages, and redemptive teleologies, one begins the process of inquiry into the status of meaning and value unencumbered by a desire for origin or the burdensome inevitability of epistemological, political, or theological destination.

In this critical space opened by Nietzsche, one needs to attend to the multiplicity, simultaneity, and undecideability of origins and ends. Within paracritical inquiry, this endeavor posits an anoriginal origin that is viewed, from the beginning, as primordial radicality; in other words, paracritical inquiry suspends origin as genesis and end as apocalypse. If we look again to Nietzsche's philosophy as a "source" of postmodern thought, not only is the beginning of artistic and critical enterprises *post*poned, the end is *post*poned as well:

> They place that which comes at the end – unfortunately! for it ought not to come at all! – namely, the "highest concepts", which means the most general, the emptiest concepts, the last smoke of an evaporating reality, in the beginning, as the beginning. This again is nothing but their way of showing reverence: the higher may not grow out of the lower, may not have grown at all. … That which is last, thinnest and emptiest is put first as cause in itself, as *ens realissimum*.[1]

One sees with a certain degree of clarity the effects of this double postponement of end and beginning, meaning and value, in the writings of Nietzsche that emphasize the essentially hermeneutic dimension of human knowledge of the world [*die den Menschen etwas anghet*]. The world, we learn, is merely an autobiographical world, largely unwritten for Nietzsche's progeny, today's postmodern thinkers and writers. Nietzsche's ambivalence toward *Ursprungsphilosophie* has carried over into the contemporary anti-foundationalist epistemologies of Jacques Derrida, Gilles Deleuze, and Jean-François Lyotard.[2] It is this radicality of thought that positions Nietzsche as a pre-postmodernist, to be followed by the phenomenologists and, later, the existentialists who questioned the presence of a delitiscent

sacred truth anchoring human life. Postmodern para/inquiry, as a form of metacritique, begins, then, with a fissuring of the language-world of intelligibility and the collapse of exclusive structurality.

Artists, philosophers, and writers in the age of postmodernism continually pay tribute to Nietzsche's thought by addressing the heterogeneity and ultimate inaccessibility of origin and end. It is because of this desultory activity that postmodernism often, and perhaps wrongly, is described as collage, eclecticism, and pastiche. To express a postmodern sensibility that goes beyond the cultural commonsense, writers and artists often disrupt and fragment the "ontos" and "telos" of their works. For example, the German artist Thomas Schütte emphasizes the contrast between nature and simulacrum. His *Schwarze Zitronen* (Black Lemons) subverts the point of origin (nature) by recreating the form in glazed black ceramic (art). His *Kirschensäule* (Cherry Column) again subverts the notion of origin by casting Classical architectural style, the triumphal column, in the everyday material of mass culture. Artists such as Schütte, in an age of postmodernism, occupy an uneasy position in relation to postmodernism in so far as the label "postmodernist artist" suggests a style directing a creative process, when, actually, it should be understood as a term descriptive of a style. Following the example set by pre-postmodernist philosophers such as Mircea Eliade, Søren Kierkegaard, André Malraux, and Friedrich Nietzsche, whom I will discuss in more detail later, today's artists easily cross disciplinary and aesthetic parameters. Painting, for instance, is not always flat and representational. Literature is not always a still-life in words. In the age of postmodernism, the world of imagination is not cast as simply an analog to the world of nature. Postmodern works of art, and literary texts especially, demonstrate this ambiguous link that is forged between language and the/a real world. Just as painting is not always flat and literature is not always mimetic, philosophical inquiry, too, occasionally disobeys the hard rules of the discipline, namely the syllogism.

> In all his works, Carroll examines the differences between events, things, and states of affairs. But the entire first half of *Alice* still seeks the secret of the events and of the becoming unlimited which they imply, in the depths of the earth, in dug out shafts and holes which plunge beneath, and in the mixture of bodies which interpenetrate and coexist.[3]

Gilles Deleuze's reading of Carroll, clearly showing an indebtedness to Nietzsche's critique of philosophy, describes the ways in which depth gives way to surface. Ordinarily, if one follows Deleuze's practice of reading, a literary and philosophical text usually has a surface and depth; the depth is where meaning allegedly resides. Alice's movement below the surface, into the underground of language, does not, for Deleuze, necessarily place her in the proximity of meaning. It is, he argues, the opposite. As Alice moves deeper, meaning becomes less available. It is on this point that Deleuze introduces the concept of *laterality*, which speaks to the location of meaning in the age of postmodernism. One does not move into the depths of meaning; one moves across meanings: "Events are like crystals, they become and grow only out of the edges, or on the edge."[4]

LITERARY AND POLITICAL SURFACES

While Deleuzean "laterality" seems appropriate to a discussion of the aesthetic dimension of

the literary text, what does it mean for the ever-present political dimension of the literary text? Does Deleuzean "laterality" simply cast off politics, leaving it aside as an unaddressable sphere? One can, I will argue, carry Deleuzean "laterality" into the present to more fully elaborate the politics–aesthetics of reading. Approaching the Deleuzean "revolutionary character" of texts is no small matter in postmodernism. The generic criticism of postmodernism, poststructuralism, and deconstruction has been that each and all mount assaults upon reality resulting in a dismissal of "politics." Only the first part of the criticism, I believe, has value. Postmodernism, poststructuralism, and deconstruction do, in fact, assault the *concept* of reality from differing philosophical directions. One can say with a certain degree of accuracy that these discourses do indeed combine to problematize the epistemological and linguistic character of the reality upon which any politics is based. This does not mean that postmodernism, poststructuralism, and deconstruction are necessarily antipolitical or apolitical. Rather, these discourses recast the conceptualizations of "reality" and "politics." The consequences for politics remain to be seen.

LATERALIZING POLITICAL LITERATURE

In his recent scholarly endeavor, aptly entitled *The Novel*, André Brink reconsiders the history of the genre by taking into account the perspective, dominant from "Cézanne onwards," that "the medium is the message," which is to say that language is central in the construction, not the representation, of reality. At times tempted to make the claim that all novels are postmodern, Brink investigates the notion of the "primacy of language as language," with

Joyce's *Finnegans Wake* the exemplary model. While *The Novel* advances a well-thought-out postmodern theory of language and narrative, it is Brink's creative work that is most relevant to our topic of para/inquiry. The burdensome desire for an originary origination that directs the history of the novel, according to Brink, is captured quite succinctly in the Preface to his novel *The Cape of Storms: The First Life of Adamastor*, in which he writes that the "distinctions between *was* and *wasn't* are rather blurred."[5] It is worth mentioning that in both spheres, scholarly and creative, Brink, known as a political writer, addresses much of the criticism that has been leveled against postmodernism for its supposed apolitical nature. He argues that Derrida's now famous-line that "there is nothing outside the text" [*Il n'y a pas d'hors-texte*] was wrongly taken to mean that the world is inconsequential. It also was mistakenly read to mean that intellectual endeavors were inconsequential. In stating his proposition, Brink reminds us, Derrida was arguing that there is not a transcendent element that settles, as a matter of adjudication, the issue of interpretation. Or, in other words, there is not an ultimate or transcendent signified that gathers all signifiers (meaning and value) beneath it.

In *The Cape of Storms: The First Life of Adamastor*, André Brink interrupts the beginning of his own narrative, the form of the novel, and the reader's processes of interpretation, by directing attention to the Derridean infinity of anterior narrative moments which "begins," or has already "begun," his writing: "in which, after some critical remarks about early French and Portuguese interpretations of Adamastor, the narrator proposes the terms of his contract with the reader."[6] Thus "begins" the peculiar introduction to *The Cape of Storms*, in which Brink divulges to the reader that the motivation behind his recent literary "venture" is a "nagging question" concerning the possible existence of an "Urtext" – an unwritten cosmogonic myth, some "raw material," which may have informed the sixteenth-century

European story of Adamastor. According to Brink, Adamastor the Titan, whose body formed the "jagged outcrop of the Cape Peninsula," appears for the first time in Rabelais's *Pantagruel*, some time after European explorers made their first contact with the people of southern Africa.[7] Brink's fascination with the possibility of an unwritten Urtext linking together Rabelais's and Camões's Adamastor leads him to ponder the ramifications of a cultural and historical synthesis of Europe and southern Africa through the fragmented structure of myth and the subjectivity of an immortal prophet.

The seemingly eternal and coalescing promise of an available cross-cultural cosmogony compels Brink to begin with beginnings. His narrative sets an immortal prophet and a possible unwritten Urtext that shapes the myth of Adamastor alongside the story of Christ's death and resurrection. This competing structure of sacrality is brought to the African continent by the explorers, thus suggesting that one could reveal through comparative myth a place and moment of origin, or, at least, first contact between European explorers and the people of southern Africa. This profound opposition between the shared Urtext and the unshared world comes to expression in Brink's novel through the articulation and designation of sacred space around the presence of an eternal hero: "Our fear turned to jubilation. With our own eyes we had witnessed that, far from desecrating the grave, these people also respected our Great Hunter; so there was nothing to fear anymore."[8] Brink's Adamastor, the person of T'Kama, goes on to tell the story of that first contact between Vasco de Gama and his men on their way to or from the East.

The novel seems to play back for the reader, time and time again, the urgent desire for origins and destinations in literature and myth. The first contact between the European explorers and the people of the African continent is more than an historical moment to be frozen in time; it extends beyond that actual moment of seeing the Other for the first time. In many ways, the first contact is preceded by the *concept* of contact.

BEGINNING WITH PARAHUMANS

> This island's mine, by Sycorax my mother
> Which thou tak'st from me.

(Shakespeare, The Tempest, I. ii. 331–2)

Literature, critics will argue, offers us the ability to view the Other from the vantage point of the European explorers. Rabelais's monster and all monsters who represent the negative moment of Western civilization, e.g. Caliban in Shakespeare's *The Tempest*, introduce to the reader, through a breach of "decorum," the order of civilization:

> Thou most lying slave,
> Whom stripes may move, not kindness! I have us'd thee
> (Filth as thou art) with human care, and log'd thee
> In mine own cell, till thou didst seek to violate
> The honor of my child.[9]

Prospero reverses the moral force of Caliban's complaint much in the same way he reverses the winds and nature, causing cataclysmic disaster. Prospero's control of nature is a

metaphor for his control of and over the beginning or the Cosmos. This, of course, includes the categories of the human and the non-human. Within the play, Caliban is a necessary monster against whom Prospero must construct an identity. The winds that Prospero is able to conjure, through good magic, deconstruct the naturalness of nature and, by implication, morality. Prospero is caught in a tension between the human, the superhuman, and the non-human. Caliban's moral complaint, which is more an appeal through humanity, calls for a response that Prospero cannot readily provide without revealing his own and civilization's contradictions. What Caliban's complaint demands, however, is a clear definition of "humanity," a definition possible for Prospero only through a process of negation. Ironically, it is Miranda, the innocent child, who in this crisis comes to her father's rhetorical aid and who, too, invokes her own reversal of Caliban's complaint by delineating, without reflection, the origins of human nature and the non-human:

> Abhorred slave,
> Which any print of goodness will not take,
> Being capable of all ill! I pitied thee,
> Took pains to make thee speak, taught thee each hour
> One thing or other. When thou didst not, savage,
> Know thine own meaning, but wouldst gabble like
> A thing most brutish, I endow'd thy purposes
> With words that made them known: but thy vile race
> (Though thou didst learn) had that in't which good natures
> Could not abide to be with; therefore wast thou

Deservedly confin'd into this rock,
Who hadst deserv'd more than a prison.[10]

Miranda, the supposed innocent, chastises Caliban for his essential vile nature in such a way as to suggest the availability of a coherent moral code predicated upon the implicit "good natures" of all humans. She describes how she attempted to impart this nature to Caliban through the transformation of "gabble" into ordered language; her *mission civilitrice* is apparent in her efforts to bring Caliban into humanity through this order of language. Her reversal of Caliban's complaint is not altogether irreversible, in the sense that both Caliban and Prospero step outside the order of nature in their own unique ways. Miranda's difficulty is in preventing her venomous attack on Caliban (depicting him as the monster who is outside of nature) from spilling over onto her father, who also defies the order of language through his incantations. Miranda's order is sustained by what lies outside of it, in this case the "vile race" to which Caliban belongs. The integrity of human nature is sustained by that which, in effect, lies outside of it: Caliban.

Caliban's presence, his role as monster, and his enslavement on the island provide the opportunities for moral reversibility. This reversibility, however, is not ending. Morality is dismantled, not by a higher morality, but by the lack of a higher morality, to which Caliban appeals for justice. Prospero's moral ascent to the sacred is a descent or a lateral move into an alternate structure – in this case, magic. For Prospero to become more civilized he must become more brutal. The impossibility of ascent to a higher plane, the sacred, results in a frustration and brutality which presses upon the Other to define, via the negative, the human center. Like Caliban on the island, the Other of Western discourse must become for the same

26

ever more vile in order to sustain the idea of order, righteousness, good natures, and community through civilization.

If one then returns to Brink's Adamastor as a contemporary manifestation of this civilizing mission, the residue of Shakespeare's Caliban is apparent. Shakespeare's Caliban is closely connected to the Adamastor by certain discursive strands. Both represent the repressed passions in civilization which exceed civilization. The sexuality of Caliban and T'Kama are held in suspension around an ambiguous civilized sexuality. In this sense, the parahuman–parasacred coupling is both a site of oppression and a site of liberation. The civilized can be sexual only as it draws from the savage the necessary energies of sexual expression. Both Caliban and T'Kama are within the discourse of civilization, even while they are unaware of it. T'Kama, in particular, is more uncivilized than Caliban in so far as he is completely alien to the explorers. A mark of the civilized is language, and Caliban clearly had been instructed in its use by the good Miranda:

The problem was that it was impossible to talk to the visitors. I had the distinct impression that they knew nothing resembling a language. They could utter sounds, but these were quite meaningless, like the chattering of birds. So perhaps they were a kind of bird after all. However, we tried to communicate with them through gestures and after a while they began to respond in the same way.[11]

Brink reverses the context for deciding upon what is civilized. T'Kama, unlike Caliban, becomes the bearer of discourse, and it is the visitors who are non-communicative and, perhaps, not human but a "kind of bird." Human identity is confused upon first contact. It is the civilized who gabble and the uncivilized who have language, or so it seems.

MASTER NARRATIVES AND OTHERNESS

The beginning sought, for example, by André Brink in *The Cape of Storms: The First Life of Adamastor*, and to some extent by Shakespeare, is actually the first human life of Adamastor or the monster. That is, the first life before both became a parahuman life, a monstrosity, entering into language and dialogue with the civilized. Just as Caliban is charged with an attempted sex crime, so too is T'Kama. The difference, however, is that T'Kama's crime is in his desire to penetrate the West, to have sexual intercourse with the Western woman. His desire is deferred by his own penis which is too large and makes intercourse, for a while at least, impossible. He is unable to penetrate because of his excess. In order for him to have sexual relations he must undergo a resizing, a re-education in which he himself must first be penetrated.

SACRALITY AND COLONIALISM

This first contact between the European explorers and the people of the Cape is brought to us through Adamastor's textured memory and his vivid recollection of the demarcation of the sacred. Brink compares and explores Adamastor's death and rebirth with the Christ story. The

overlapping of myths continues throughout the novel into other comparative stories of power and ultimacy. Adamastor's challenging of the gods, for instance, resonates particularly with Prometheus's act of defiance. The recurrence of a cosmogonic myth of human rebellion carries the reader through a series of multi-narrative labyrinths. Adamastor's voices, especially that of the person of T'Kama, express the feeling that his people need not fear the "bearded-men" because both people share a sense of the sacred – Heitisi-Eibib's cairn and Golgotha both represent the *axis mundi*. In the course of the novel, however, T'Kama learns that his particular notion of the universality of the sacred is entirely wrong. To his chagrin he discovers that, while the European explorers and the people of the Cape designate something as sacred, sacrality does not come to material expression in exclusively one form.[12] It does not necessarily coalesce around one and only one manifestation or hierophany, nor does it necessarily emanate from the same source. In many ways, Brink's novel can be read as a religio-political allegory, telling the story of the sacred through the history of European exploration and colonialism.

Crosses, symbols of the power and ultimacy of the West, transform into politico-ideological formations and, subsequently, into political practices: the "Holy Cross" and what it symbolizes, to the European explorers, subsumed all of humanity. It is, and has been in the name of this universality, configured by a Christian cosmology which lays claim to the power to unfold the sacrality of the Other and render it intelligible. The Christ story, with its emphasis on death and resurrection, seems upon first reading to resonate with the story of the savior–hero Heitisi-Eibib and his many dyings without death. And, yet it is not the same dying; nor is it the same returning to life. Do these two stories, then, actually tell the same story of the sacred? Is there but one sacred and one story with variation? This is the question that drives Brink's narrative.

The Western religio-philosophical tradition has a desire for such a universality, and, for the most part, has answered "yes" to these questions, pointing to the very essence of the human person (as illustrated by the suffering of the hero or eternal prophet) as evidence of this one story. However, Adamastor's death and Prometheus's binding were sentences of a tyrant god. In both cases, the myths express a resistance to tyranny (spiritual as well as political) and foretell its end in revolution. This is unlike the Christ story, in which the death of Jesus is not typically read as the culminating act of a tyrannical God; instead, Jesus's death, is an act of obedience, affirming the eternality of the Cosmos through one God. Brink depicts this totalizing dynamic in which the "Other's" sacred is (re)valued and subsumed within Christian cosmology, universal obedience.

This totalizing dynamic of which Brink attempts to find the origin has often been associated with the Western habit of exploration. One is left to speculate as to the cause of this habit which results in the explorer leaving home, as it were, and "discovering other people." Brink's literary venture puts us somewhat closer to understanding this phenomenon by telling the story of contact from the other point of view – that of the one who did not leave home. This imaginative undertaking strives to forestall a desire for cosmogony and the prerequisite of a temporal subject in favor of a subjectivity not bound by history's temporal or cultural condition. Wandering through Brink's narrative, the reader finds that it represents a challenge to the concept of humanity as the unifying principle of the cosmology. The question of the Urtext and the multiple subjectivity of Adamastor pose an interesting alternative narrative to the story of first contact. Where there were once clear convergences in the form

of cosmogonic myths, expressing what is irreducibly human, unique to each and common to all, there is a point of divergence from the designation of the sacred. This point of divergence challenges the presumption of the universal human person in the Western religio-philosophical tradition by presenting the following proposition: If we do not share the same sacred, we are not the same.

Brink's retexturing of the myth and suspension of a shared cosmogony, although certainly not alone in this respect, depicts a moment of crisis in the European identity; he writes a story that is a reversal in the way that the West thinks of cosmology. The historical trajectory of the Western religio-philosophical tradition favors a cosmogony build upon sameness, and this privileging has worked toward defining and articulating the conceptual boundaries that frame and define the unity of the sacred, as well as elucidating the essential underpinnings of human existence across time, cultural context, and geography. Cosmology leads to a convergence of difference that celebrates the principle of sameness in order to avoid the dehiscing effects of difference; postmodern para/inquiry, however, with its relevance to literature and culture, respects these differences. The valuing of convergences has come not only to define the Western tradition, but to pre-empt the discussion of difference from becoming part of establishing the frame for conceptualizing the complexity of the human mode of being. This insistence upon the exclusion of divergences, the erasing of difference, and the inclusion of convergences, the privileging of sameness, takes shape today in the on-going tensions in the age of postmodernism.

CHAPTER 3

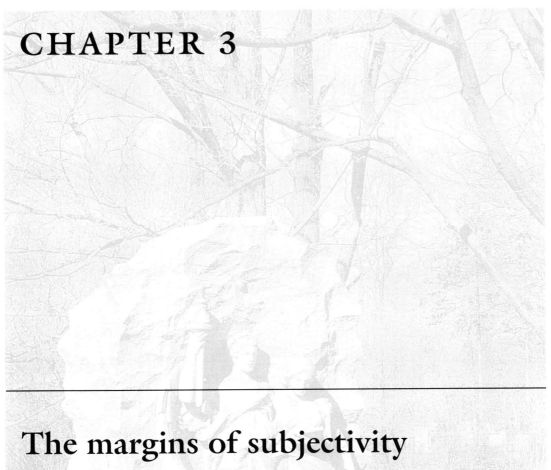

The margins of subjectivity and culture

The aspects of things that are most important for us are hidden because of their simplicity and familiarity. (One is unable to notice something – because it is always before one's eyes.) The real foundations of his inquiry do not strike a man at all. Unless that fact has at some time struck him – And this means: we fail to be struck by what, once seen, is most striking and powerful.

(Ludwig Wittgenstein, *Philosophical Investigations*)

A text is not a text unless it hides from the first comer [*Un texte n'est un texte que s'il cache au premier regard*], from the first glance, the laws of its composition and the rules of its game [*la règle de son jeu*]. A text remains, moreover, forever imperceptible. Its law and its rules are not, however, harbored in the inaccessibility of a secret; it is simply that they can never be booked, in the *present*, into anything that could rigorously be called a perception.

And hence, perceptually and essentially, they run the risk of being definitively lost. Who will ever know of such disappearances? [*Qui saura jamais telle disparition?*]

(Jacques Derrida, "Plato's Pharmacy," *Dissemination*)

LISTENING FOR THE ORIGIN

The silence of the Sphinx conjures up romantic expectations of receiving an answer to the ageless question: "Why do you live?" Mark Tansey's depiction of the eternal human quest for authenticity presents this secret of the ages within a postmodern context that does much

31

Figure 3.1 Elihu Vedder's *Questioner of the Sphinx*, 1863 (Oil on canvas, 36 x 41¾ inches. Bequest of Mrs Martin Brimmer. Reproduced with the permission of the Museum of Fine Arts, Boston, MA)

Figure 3.2 Mark Tansey's *Secret of the Sphinx* (*Homage to Elihu Vedder*), **1984 (Oil on canvas, 60 x 65 inches. Reproduced with the permission of the Curt Marcus Gallery, New York. © Mark Tansey 1985)**

32

more than simply lament the absence of the sacred or scorn the lack of authenticity in postmodern life. Mark Tansey, for whom the lack of authenticity in the postmodern age is a significant theme, conveys this sense of urgency surrounding individual and collective authenticity in a number of his works dealing with the epistemological abyss that exists between the real and the represented.[1] Tansey's *Secret of the Sphinx (Homage to Elihu Vedder)* (1984), for instance, points to Vedder's *The Questioner of the Sphinx* (1863) in both style and subject. Vedder's oil on canvas depicts a man with his ear firmly pressed up against the lips of the Sphinx, yearning to hear the sacred secret. Tansey's 1984 revisiting of the issue places technology (a recording device and accessories) between the questioner's ear and the Sphinx's lips. Tansey's audio-relay interrupts Vedder's implied immediacy and expresses the postmodern notion that the secret, if there is a secret to be heard at all, is mediated by some extra-human apparatus. There is not, as Tansey makes clear, an instance of pure transmission from ancient past to the here and now. In a Derridean sense, one could say of the Sphinx that "its law and rules are not harbored in the inaccessibility of a secret" (*Dissemination*, 63); or, in a Lyotardian sense, that the secret of the Sphinx does not come in the form of a grand narrative. As a result, our postmodern sensibilities must contend with the lasting illusion of purity contained within the Sphinx. Unlike Vedder's original, Tansey's recasting of the existential crisis as an epistemological crisis calls into question the possibility of achieving an authentic existence through a supposedly unmediated transmission of the sacred from the ancient past to present humanity.

AUTHENTICITY

The Sphinx has symbolized the possibility not only of authentic individual existence through the transmission of pure knowledge in myth and literature across the ages, but the possibility of authentic *communal* existence. Sophocles's Œdipus, for instance, must conquer the Sphinx by solving its riddle before he is able to establish himself as a man of knowledge and the ruler of Thebes. Just as in the ancient myths in which the Sphinx symbolizes both chaos and order, so does it serve us today. In his 1967 novella *The Beggar*, the Egyptian writer Naguib Mahfouz introduces us to Omar, a dissolute man who attempts to soothe a festering existential wound by regularly returning to the Sphinx and the pyramids after nights of heavy drinking, to have illicit sex with dancers. Ultimately, he seeks intercourse of another kind – a communion with an ancient past that is represented by the Sphinx. He experiences a profound loss of meaning in his individual existence, and in the existence of his community as well. He is, in many respects, a postmodern man betrayed by his own desires for reconciliation within a transcendent order. He asks, despairingly: "If you really wanted me, why did you desert me?"[2] The overwhelming question for Omar is: What does the secret hold? The ancient past seems to withhold the remedy for the corruption found in everyday life. Omar's Sphinx and pyramids taunt him and his community with their unrelenting silence:

> The desert sands, clothed in darkness, hid the whispers, as numberless as the grains, of past generations – their hopes, their suffering, and all their last questions. There is no pain without a cause, something told him, and somewhere this enchanted, ephemeral moment will endure.

33

> Here, I am beseeching the silence to utter, for if that happened, all would change. If only the sands would loosen their hidden powers, and liberate me from this oppressive impotence.[3]

The sacrality of life that is symbolically expressed in Omar's marriage, his children, his love of poetry, is substituted with illicit sexual encounters, business deals, and an obsession with failing health. Omar consistently substitutes what supposedly is sacred in his life with what is profane. He seeks ultimacy and meaning in decadence:

> He felt the glances of the other women who'd gone with him, night after night. As Warda smiled, he muttered, "I didn't desire them."
> She raised her eyebrows.
> "I knew them all, without exception, but there was never any desire."
> "Then why?"
> "Hoping the divine moment would unlock the answer."
> She said resentfully, "How cruel you were. You men don't believe in love unless we disbelieve in it."
> "Perhaps, but that's not my problem."
> The scent of orange blossoms drifting from the dark fields suggested secret worlds of delight. Feeling suddenly light and unfettered, he asked fervently, "Tell me Warda, why do you live?"
> She shrugged her shoulders and finished her drink, but when he repeated the question, he was so clearly in earnest that she replied, "Does that question have any meaning?"[4]

The question he asks his dancer is the question that plagues his own existence and the existence of the community. In the end, however, Omar remains a beggar for meaning and value. The secret is never released to him and an authentic existence is never within his grasp. Not only does Warda refuse to answer his question meaningfully, but she allows the question to fall in on itself: the question, we see through her eyes, has no meaning.

The implication of Omar's desire for authenticity takes on a new meaning in light of postmodernism. Mahfouz, however unintentionally, has captured a sense of postmodernism that, as a philosophical venture, is contrary to what Lévi-Strauss defined as the "ultimate goal of the human sciences" – the constitution of man. The postmodern dissolution of man or the human subject is a fracturing of the center, the megaliths, the structures of language and culture which, over the centuries in Western civilization, have provided a space for the sacred and have grounded the authentic individual and collective identities that flow from it; or, as expressed in T.S. Eliot's *The Waste Land*, "These fragments I have shored against my ruins."[5] It is precisely modernism's fragmentation and subsequent desire for, and firm belief in, reunification that postmodernism oddly commemorates as the immemorial – the absence present in ruins and the secret that is never divulged by the Sphinx. The fragments of the (im)memorials of the past and present point in the direction of a center that the human subject has made its own by a process of unification, individualization, and internalization by dislocating the sacred from the outside of existence (an object-dominated world) to human consciousness (a subject-dominated world).

This center regularly appears in Western philosophy as the bi-partition of the world, the realm of the Forms and the realm of sensible things; we find the transcendent sacred expressed in the profane; we find also the sacred, representing power and ultimacy,

34

anchoring the subject and, in doing so, giving meaning and value to human existence. This dialectical separation that is posited at the center of human existence comes to fuller expression in René Descartes's seminal philosophical treatise *Meditations on First Philosophy (In Which the Existence of God and the Distinction of the Soul from the Body Are Demonstrated)*. As Charles E. Winquist notes in *Desiring Theology*, modern philosophy "begins with a search for roots or foundations of knowledge."[6] This search for knowledge, however, finds its beginning in the contaminate of radical doubt, a contaminate that Descartes and modern philosophy were unable to purify with a transcendent order or universal human subjectivity. Winquist goes on to add:

> God is a figuration within subjective discourse that disrupts hegemony of the subject over all experience. God means what discourse is not. The conceiving of God is an argument against idealistic solipsism. It enfranchises consideration of that which is other than subjectivity from within subjectivity. This sense of the other is a theological exigency of the mind. Talk of God is incorrigible to the assertion of subjective dominance.[7]

Descartes ends, as Winquist points out, with a "world smaller than the world that he began with."[8] Descartes inverts the world of objects and, in so doing, expresses the "new" world as a function of God, which is actually an extension of subjectivity. In this logical arrangement, the world and the concept of "Other" exist as thinly disguised projections of the sovereign subject:

The fact that I exist and have an idea in me of a perfect entity – that is, God – conclusively entails that God does in fact exist.

All that's left is to explain how I have gotten my idea of God from Him. I have not taken it in through my senses; it has never come to me unexpectedly as the ideas of sensible things do when those things affect (or seem to affect) my external organs of sense. Nor have I made the idea myself; I can't subtract from it or add to it. The only other possibility is that the idea is innate in me, like my idea of myself.[9]

Descartes's proof for both the existence of God and the existence of the human subject, as we have seen, inaugurates modern philosophy's attempted reconciliation of the real and the represented; or, within the history of Western thought, the resolution of Plato's realm of the Forms with the realm of sensible things. Unlike the newly formed modern world of Descartes, the postmodern world is marked by the failure to recuperate the fragments of ruin, to reunite the subject and the world; we cannot help but to notice, after revisiting Descartes, our postmodern whirlpool and the absence of a sacred center that is indicative of our age.[10] To pull us further away from the transcendent and closer to a postmodern condition, we have before us the impossiblity of certainty of any kind, and the universality of human subjectivity.

Within this postmodern condition there is silence from the Sphinx, and we are left, like Mahfouz's Omar, wondering what, if anything, it meant to be possessed by universality. In the paralogical network of postmodernism, neither the sacred nor the universal human subject remain intact. The sacred is in ruins and the possessed and possessing subjects are diffused across the plane of language and uncertainties. Our postmodern uncertainty, which leads to

anxiety concerning meaning and value, delivers us over to, and not from, the concept of parasacrality.

PARASACRALITY: *PAGUS/POLIS*

It is this quixotic fantasy of returning to the sacred and the eternal foundation of Western civilization that begins our current postmodern quest. Since the sacred has failed us, we now search for the para/sacred, or that which finds a place around or alongside that of the sacred or the residue of an alternate power and an alternate ultimacy we cannot yet name. The parasacred of postmodernity continues from the frayed end(s) of a modernist aesthetic revealed in an artistic, historical, philosophical, political, or religious process of synthesis. It is a synthesizing process marked by multiple and unsynthesizable beginnings and endings which spontaneously occur as incisions, tears, or punctures in the external limiting surface of language. Derrida's "Plato's Pharmacy" attends to this unweaving of language:

> The dissimulation of the woven texture can in any case take centuries to undo its web: a web that envelops a web, undoing the web of centuries; reconstituting it too as an organism, indefinitely regenerating its own tissue behind the cutting trace [*la trace coupante*], the decision of each reading [*la décision de chaque lecture*].[11]

Such an incision, tear, or puncture is an arbitrary wounding of the discursive tissue indicating the incorrigibility of language's depth, its ideational boundaries, the directional signs marking the proper path to the sacred, as well as the way of erring. The incision, tear or puncture begins with Mahfouz's question: Why do you live? The parasacred interrupts the structural integrity of authentic existence (individual and social) by first drawing attention to the guiding assumptions which traditionally have led inquiry in the direction of the sacred.

In the West, the cultural expression of the human mode of being requires an incontrovertible definition (scientific or religious) of human subjectivity and, by implication, a definition of Otherness or of some other human against which to measure "humanness". Jacques Derrida, in "Plato's Pharmacy,"[12] explains this doubleness contained within definition by drawing together the ambiguities of the word *pharmakon*, which in ancient Greek means both cure and poison. The doubleness of the *pharmakon*, its status as both cure and poison, reflects the organizational logic of early Athenian democracy, which needed the negative instantiation of the city to form an ideal city:

> The city's body *proper* thus reconstitutes its unity, closes around the security of its inner courts, gives back to itself the word that links it with itself within the confines of the agora, by violently excluding from its territory the representative of an external threat or aggression [*en excluant violemment de son territoire le représentant de la menace ou de l'agression extérieure*]. That representative represents the otherness of the evil [*l'altérité du mal*] that comes to affect or infect the inside by unpredictably breaking into it. Yet the representative of the outside is none the less *constituted*, regularly granted its place by the community, chosen, kept, fed, etc., in the very heart of the inside. These parasites were as a matter of course domesticated by the living organism that housed them at its expense. The Athenians regularly maintained a number of

> degraded and useless beings at the public expense; and when any calamity, such as plague, drought, or famine, befell the city, they sacrificed two of these outcasts as scapegoats [*comme boucs émissaires*].[13]

For the ancient Athenians, what was not a part of the city proper (the *polis*) was a form of contaminate (the *pagus*). The *pagus*, or the pagan within the city body, continually threatened to undo what Athenian citizens had assembled. And yet, as Derrida indicates, the *polis* needed the *pagus*; the citizens needed the pagan to give definition to the sacred through sacrifice, or expression and meaning to the conceptual structures which ordered their community. Just as the *pharmakon* is both cure and poison and *hagios* is both pure and polluted, the sacred (*le sacré*) is simultaneously the holy and the accursed. This doubleness comes to expression in the modern world by way of historical reflection and re-enactment. Just as the ancient world constructed an Otherness to define its sacred, the modern world has constructed its Other. The city *proper* [*le corps propre de la cité*] can be manufactured along with an Other, a pagan force, the para/sacred, to reconstitute its continuity with the ancient past and the sacred secret it holds.

NEGATING THE OTHER

The notion of the city set beside itself is best illustrated by the "White City" of the Columbian Exposition of 1893. The World Parliament of Religions, convened in 1893 in connection with the Columbian Exposition, was determined to further encourage academic studies of the world's religions and unite those religions under Christianity:

> To unite all Religion against all irreligion; to make the Golden Rule the basis of this union; to present to the world … the substantial unity of many religions in the good deeds of the Religious Life; to provide for a World Parliament of Religions, in which their common aims and grounds of unity may be set forth, and the marvelous Religious progress of the Nineteenth Century be reviewed.[14]

It is the construction of unity, via the ancient past and Otherness, in relation to the modern ideal or proper city, which gives rise to many humanistic questions today, much in the same way, for example, as it did in Chicago in 1893 – the ultimate manufactured city, the White City. In this sense, the Chicago Exposition serves as an illustration of the emergence of the parasacred.

Chroniclers of the Chicago Exposition note their fascination with the human achievements of the Western world. Behind the neoclassical façades of plaster, cement, and jute fiber were electric stoves, electric lights, telephones, and what were to become the everyday appliances of the twentieth century. Not only did the Columbian Exposition celebrate technological achievements, but it demonstrated something of the extent, the promise, of the Western technological mode of existence and the dominance of a Western mode of subjectivity. The neoclassical architecture brought the Exposition-goers back in "time" to the secrets and origins of Western civilization. The past and present, as it was intended, came together in one moment of transmitting the sacred from the ancient past to the present.

At the same time as the Exposition's neoclassical *faux* structures of plaster and wood housed the achievements of the Western world, there were other enclosures there with other humans who were not entirely participatory in or celebratory of this civilizing power. The exhibits on the Exposition's Midway Plaisance featured ethnological studies of the non-Western world, the conquered, which were supervised by Harvard anthropologist Fredric Ward Putnam. F.W. Putnam, in attempting to bring together two worlds, hired as the organizer Sol Bloom who, unlike his contemporaries, wrote: "I came to realize that a tall, skinny chap from Arabia with the talent for swallowing swords expressed a culture which to me was on a higher plane than the one demonstrated by a group of earnest Swiss peasants who passed their day making cheese and milk chocolate."[15] Ward's assistant Harlan Ingersoll Smith was less generous, and perhaps more attuned with the thinking of his time, when he stated that the ethnological exhibits "from the first to the last … will be arranged to teach a lesson; to show the advancement of evolution of man."[16]

The White City, or the "whited sepulchre" as Frederick Douglass and Ida Barnett Wells named it in their essay "The Reason Why the Colored American is Not in the World's Columbian Exposition,"[17] symbolized the center of humanity; and the neoclassical architecture, recalling the Golden Age of Greece, created the sense of a celestial city – a sacred place in which all humanity, even those thought to be not yet suitably evolved, could partake of the essence of being human. The sacrality of the Exposition's Grand Basin and the Midway held in tension a peculiar and unsteady dialectic. The Grand Basin's sacrality was dependent upon the "unholy" Midway. What this sacrality, with its totalizing discourses, attempted to suppress was actually the para/sacrality of the Midway – that which exists around and outside of the sacred. In an effort to include the achievements of African-

Americans, for example, August 25, 1893 was designated "Colored Peoples' Day." This particular day marked, and to some extent reaffirmed, the sacrality of the White City by including "African-Americans only in the racist space afforded them by white America in general." August 25 was white America's "Colored Peoples' Day," replete with all the hatred that late nineteenth-century racism offered. As the gates opened, *Puck* magazine's cartoonist Frederick Burr Opper provided "Darkies' Day at the Fair," a series of caricatures that depicted black Americans in the most hateful of racial stereotypes. Ironically, later that day, amid taunts and jeers, Frederick Douglass delivered his famous speech "The Race Problem in America." In this speech, Douglass firmly stated that "there is no Negro problem. The problem is whether the American people have loyalty enough, honor enough, patriotism enough, to live up to their own constitution."[18] It was the "enough" of Douglass's message which drew out the sense that what is sacred for America, what is ultimate, is incomplete without the parasacred of black America. The speech called into question the configuration of the ideal or proper city and, at the same time, the flawed notion that there is but one – shared – world.

If one were to have asked the question "What does it mean to be human?" in the context of the 1893 Columbian Exposition, the answer certainly would have been "To be white and Western." The "White City," the "white elephant," even the "whited sepulchre," identify the power of whiteness with civilization and humanity. In "The Reason Why," however, Barnett-Wells and Douglass continually point to another experience of the world, one which, at the time, escaped the categories of the Exposition's directors. Frederick Douglass, in particular, addresses this notion of the unshared world by pointing to his own former life as a slave in the South and the legacy of slavery that persisted at the Columbian Exposition:

38

He was a marketable commodity. His money value was regulated like any other article; it was increased or decreased according to his perfections or imperfections as a beast of burden.

Chief Justice Taney truly described the condition of our people when he said in the Dred Scott decision, that they were supposed to have no rights which white men were bound to respect. White men could shoot, hang, burn, whip and starve them to death with impunity. They were themselves made to feel themselves as outside the pale of all civil and political institutions. The masters' power of them was complete and absolute. ... So when it is asked why we are excluded from the World's Columbian Exposition, the answer is Slavery.[19]

Douglass's invocation of the horrors of slavery in his text must be read in the context of 1893, at a time when slavery was still very much a part of living memory:

The life of a Negro slave was never held sacred in the estimation of the people of that section of the country in the time of slavery, and the abolition of slavery against the will of the enslavers did not render a slave's life more sacred.[20]

Douglass's analysis of American culture, through the event of the Columbian Exposition, raises the issue of a nation's identity. An individual and a community are forced into an alliance by the impetus to unify differences under the sacred. As Douglass points out, the forming of a unified nation after abolition did not encompass the lives of black Americans. The White City, for Douglass, was more than the Columbian Exposition itself: it was a cultural logic made operational by the instantiation of homogeneous origin and *telos* via sacrality.

Just as both Tansey's listener and Mahfouz's Omar search for individual authenticity through the sacred, so does the community. The Columbian Exposition, I believe, illustrates this rather well. The construction of individual subjectivity and collective subjectivity makes necessary the formation of a contaminate against which identity-formation can take place. In light of this disturbing parallel, it is important to discuss the earlier debates in cultural theory around the topic of human identity. In the section which follows, it is easy to see the stakes of the contest, which are no less than determining the definition of the human person.

THE SECRET SPOKEN: BÜRGERLICHEN WELT

> It is a form of power that makes individual subjects. There are two meanings of the word *subject*: subject to some one else by control or dependence, and tied to his own identity by a conscience or self-knowledge. Both meanings suggest a form of power which subjugates and makes subject to.
>
> (Michel Foucault, "Why Study Power?" *Power/Knowledge*)

Why study the subjugation of subjects? The answer may be found in the postmodernist re-articulation of the human person as a product of a form of power. This reassessment of humanity by cultural theorists diverged from humanistic studies in the most radical way possible. Cultural theorists advocated the view that the human person is an inscription of linguistic and social relations, while liberal humanists saw themselves as preserving the sovereignty of the human person.

For the purpose of illustrating the politico-philosophical dimensions of this debate, I turn

to a pointed lecture given by M.H. Abrams in May 1993, entitled "What Is Humanistic Criticism?", inaugurating the Heinrich and Alice Schneider Memorial Lecture Series at Cornell University.[21] Abrams's address serves to delineate the ideological and political implications of restructuring the humanistic critique in the age of postmodernism. In his lecture, Abrams first (and, I am sure, quite unexpectedly for his audience) explicates postmodern thought and then proceeds to prosecute his case against what he calls "*poststructural* conceptual schemes and interpretative practices." Having framed his indictment, Abrams ends his lecture with a simple answer to a complex question, and therein it is possible to see an enduring and, perhaps, misplaced faith in something called "common humanity": "'What is a Humanistic Criticism'? Quite simply, humanistic criticism deals with a work of literature as written by a human being, for human beings and about human beings and matters of human concern."[22] Abrams grounds his understanding or definition of the human person in two important ways. First, he posits language as a totalizable system and, more specifically, he views language as evidence of the autonomy of the human person in the creation of meaning; second, he constructs an aesthetic out of that understanding of language which unifies the world of experience for all human beings under the rubric of "common humanity," which he redefines first as "matters of human concern," and later as "tact." Abrams's "matters of human concern" come together in the way language becomes both the ground and the medium of the universalizable expression of the human mode of being in the world. Humanistic criticism, then, is two-pronged: it posits the human subject in history as totalizable – the commonality of humanness; and it posits language as having a deep and eternal structure (langue) which supports and confirms meaning within historically specific language use (parole). The alleged eternality of linguistic structures allows Abrams to fall back upon the canons of taste (tact) to verify what is and, by implication, what is not a matter of human concern – matters which, as one would predict, come to expression in canonical texts and the aesthetic sensibilities of a Swift or a Keats. In shoring up the fragments of the humanistic paradigm, Abrams turns to the writings of Wittgenstein to express, contrary to Jacques Derrida in particular and the poststructuralist conceptual schemes and practices in general, the stabilizing and unifying effects language has on human practices in the world:

> In Ludwig Wittgenstein's remarkable later writings, a special concern, in what he sometimes called our *Weltbild*, is with the primitives, the "givens" which, when understood to justify our beliefs and assertions, are the termini – the "bedrock," as he puts it, "where my spade turned." And at such endpoints of the "chain of reasons," he famously declares, "What has to be accepted, the given, is – so one could say – *forms of life*."
>
> The givens, in our "world-picture," the "substratum of all my inquiring and asserting," Wittgenstein points out, do not consist of metaphysical foundations in self-evident truths or in quasi visible presences, but of our participation in pre-existing, ongoing, shared human practices. ... Such certainties, it can be argued, function not only as the presupposition of all proofs, but as the preconditions for the development and the intelligibility of a common language.[23]

Abrams continues his reading of the later Wittgenstein in such a way as to suggest that Wittgenstein confidently proposed an irreducible reality or a common or shared human world. This, I think, misleads the reader to a great extent in that, as a reading of Wittgenstein, it seems somewhat too willing to forget the complexity of Wittgenstein's theory of language as

a game with an infinite number of possible locations for play and, perhaps more importantly in this instance, the way in which Wittgenstein understood that the "world" (an instance of infinity) is the case:

> On one of their walks in Phoenix Park, Drury mentioned Hegel: "Hegel seems to me to be always wanting to say that things which look different are really the same," Wittgenstein told him. "Whereas my interest is in showing that things which look the same are really different." He was thinking of using as a motto for his book the Earl of Kent's phrase from *King Lear* (Act I, scene iv): "I'll teach you differences."
>
> His concern was to stress life's irreducible variety. The pleasure he derived from walking in the Zoological Gardens had much to do with his admiration for the immense variety of flowers, shrubs and trees and the multitude of different species of birds, reptiles and animals. A theory which attempted to impose a single scheme upon all this diversity was, predictably, anathema to him. Darwin had to be wrong: his theory "hasn't the necessary multiplicity."[24]

This particular reading of Wittgenstein's later work by Abrams, which conflicts with Ray Monk's reading, is not altogether surprising when one considers the severe consequences of allowing the poststructuralist tendencies of Wittgenstein's texts to appear in today's discussions about the humanities. This, I think, strikes at the heart of studies in the humanities – the ideological need to contain the human by claiming on behalf of all humans a shared world. Of course, such a shared world reality raises ethical and political issues that can be explored by taking some time to re-read Wittgenstein and the humanistic paradigm's appropriation of his thought and of his reliance on the tying together of language theory and aesthetic theory in the discipline of philosophy.

The humanistic paradigm's dependence on a theory of language which stabilizes meaning across time and culture can be understood as the ongoing inquiry into the nature of meaningfulness as it relates to the conditions of a physics of language and a chaotic world. I describe this inquiry, initially, as a contest over how the discipline of philosophy in particular conceives of language as a conceptual tool for uncovering the true nature of the world, and how it then exports that understanding and further promulgates the one-to-one correspondence between the signifier and the signified (the conditions for identity and difference).

Historically, the discipline of Western philosophy has posited an idea of language as a conceptual tool which allows the philosopher to discover the substance in the word to which all the attributes of the object adhere. As Mark C. Taylor observes in the Introduction to *Deconstruction in Context* (1986), the philosophy of deconstruction is not so much a recent phenomenon as a discussion, ongoing throughout the history of philosophy, of the conditions for identity and difference, understood as an inquiry into the separation/unity of the physical and the metaphysical. The philosophies of Immanuel Kant, G.W.F. Hegel, and Edmund Husserl can be thought of as prefiguring the linguistic turn inaugurated by Ferdinand de Saussure. This linguistic turn upsets the prior understanding that the signifier and the signified are essentially linked: "[T]here are only differences with no positive terms." If we accept this, the former "substance" of the word to which all the attributes of the object adhere is no longer possible. In other words, because of Saussure's difference in identity as opposed to the identity in difference, the question concerning identity–difference in Kant is no longer

answered by the reunification of the subject and the object (the signifier and the signified) through the innate genius of the artist (the poetic *Geist*) as Abrams would suggest; the question concerning identity–difference in Hegel, who is thought to have overcome Kant's poetic *Geist*, is no longer answered by the *Geist* of the absolute knowledge or the World Spirit of the "evolving dialectic of totality";[25] and it is no longer answered by Husserl's phenomenology or the "Logos" of the phenomenon which posits the true nature of things within transcendental subjectivity. The Saussurean linguistic turn moves the question concerning identity–difference toward scientific analysis or an examination of structured relationships of signs as a linguistic system.

Like Hegel, Saussure makes a distinction between the logical structure of the *idea* of language and the historical and changing realization of that structure in everyday language (the synchronic and diachronic aspects of the language system). For Saussure, the question of identity–difference, however, is within the linguistic system as the differential nature of signs which is empty of an essential concept behind the signifier. This linguistic turn makes several concepts possible: the first is that the sign is a sign within a system of signs lacking essential meaning; the second is that meaning is, therefore, historico-linguistically produced through the play of differences; the third is that meaning-effects are constituted by the linguistic system as it exists in history. This reversal of the traditional understanding of identity–difference is, in effect, an inversion of Western philosophy, in that unity and identity (the concepts privileged by Augustine, Aquinas, Kant, Hegel, and Husserl, for instance) are no longer primary. Instead, plurality and difference are primary, and this difference in identity allows for the potential (re)structuring of the discipline of philosophy as a continued site where meaningfulness is recoverable. The issue here is the condition of humanistic studies in the wake of Saussure's difference in identity and how the grafting of the later Wittgenstein to humanism effects this (re)structuring within a postmodern age. In one sense, the grafting of the later Wittgenstein to the humanistic paradigm can be understood as the latter attempting to defend itself from the attacks mounted by deconstruction. This struggle takes place within and around the ongoing collapse of the disciplinary boundaries of the academy.

In the interdisciplinary challenges to the humanities, initiated in the wake of the conceptual and discursive dismantlings and reversals produced by Saussure's linguistic turn, one finds that none have been more threatening than that mounted by deconstruction, which, while accepting the linguistic turn inaugurated by structuralism, has re-understood and deepened its implications through an attack on the logocentrism of the entire Western philosophical tradition. This turn on the structuralist's linguistic turn has rendered it impossible any longer to speak of "concepts" or "ideas" as if they were "sovereign entities," i.e. as if they had an existence "independent" of the discursive modalities in/by which they were produced. Since, at the very historical moment of these contestatory developments, language-oriented analytic studies already held sway in academic departments of philosophy, those attempting to stave off poststructuralism's dehiscing and de-disciplining effects (and the (re)structuring and reconstitution of academic philosophical studies which must follow such a destruction) have turned more and more to the possibilities of deploying discourses of analytic philosophy and ordinary language philosophy to help in their struggle against the encroachment of poststructuralism. A major part of these defensive maneuvers has been the effort either to disown poststructuralist thought entirely, or to attempt to graft the discourses of the later Wittgenstein onto the humanistic paradigm in an attempt to stave off the challenges to the apodictic core of the humanist tradition.

42

To speak of Wittgenstein as a humanist is, in effect, to (re)write the career of Wittgenstein. The later Wittgenstein, one could argue, is made intelligible by setting it beside the early Wittgenstein in such a way as to suggest that the early Wittgensteinian texts had within them the contradictions which make the latter's deconstruction possible. A conventional reading of this dismantling can be understood in the following way: Wittgenstein saw that the *Tractatus* unraveled, as it were, when the one-to-one correspondence of word and thing ended. For Wittgenstein, the language-game superseded the truth-functional nature of language or the determinate referent. This, then, is not so much the plotting out of this transformation in Wittgenstein's thought as it is a micro-critique of the conditions or presuppositions of that transformation, and of how and why the discipline of philosophy separates and unites the earlier and later thought in order to form Wittgensteinian humanism, which acts to quarantine deconstruction to the area of language. Language, instead of existing as a free play of signs, is construed by humanistic scholars as a body – a body with self-regulatory capabilities. This body metaphor is, in fact, attributable to Wittgenstein; however, one can easily quarrel with the reading that Wittgenstein was admiring the regulatory process of the body and not the play of differences across the body itself.

Like areas of language, the various parts of the human body (language) vary in temperature (meaning) according to an extensive range of physical conditions. For instance, on an exceedingly cold afternoon the flesh on a person's exposed hand may differ in temperature from, let us say, the flesh on an unexposed foot. The assumption is that the range of difference for the body, and for language, has a normative extent which is dependent upon a quantitative relation to the whole. For the body the normative range is 98.6 degrees to 98.8 degrees; in the case of language, according to the Wittgensteinian position, it is the everyday use or civil meaning of the word (the appendage) within language (the body) as a self-enclosed system of difference which forms meaning. In the "language-game [*Sprachspiel*]," according to Wittgenstein, as the physical conditions change so does the meaning of the word:

> But how many kinds of sentences are there? Say assertion, question, and command? – There are countless kinds: countless different kinds of use of what we call "symbols," "words," "sentences" [*Es gibt unzählige solcher Arten: unzählige verschieden Arten der Verwedung alles dessen, was wir Zeichen', Worte', Sätze', nennen*]. And this multiplicity [*Mannigfaligkeit*] is not something fixed, given once for all [*ein für allemal Gegebenes*]; but new types of language [*Typen der Sprache*], new language-games [*neue Sprachspiele*], as we may say, come into existence, and others become obsolete and get forgotten.
>
> Here the term "language-game" [*Sprachspiel*] is meant to bring into prominence the fact that the speaking of language is part of an activity, or of a form of life [*Lebensform*].
>
> Reviewed the multiplicity of language-games in the following examples, and in others:
>
> Giving orders, and obeying them—
> Describing the appearance of an object, or giving its measurements—
> Constructing an object from a description (a drawing)—
> Reporting an event—
> Speculating about an event.[26]

There are countless uses or civil meanings for what we may call signs (symbols, words,

43

and sentences) and there are, correspondingly, a multiplicity of contexts in which the language-games can be played out. However, for the humanist follower of Wittgenstein, this multiplicity of meaningfulness has an altogether different effect within the language-game. "Multiplicity" and "game" seem to indicate the cohesive process of language itself. My point is that in *Philosophical Investigations* one can misappropriate Wittgenstein for the purposes of countering the dismantling effects of poststructuralist conceptual schemes. John M. Ellis, in his essay "Playing Games with Wittgenstein," illustrates this frustration with poststructuralist thought:[27]

> Deconstructive discourse, in criticism, in philosophy, or in poetry itself, undermines the referential status of language being deconstructed.

> As a mode of textual theory and analysis, contemporary *deconstruction* subverts almost everything in the tradition, putting in question received ideas of sign and language, the text, the context, the author, the reader, the role of history, the work of interpretation, and the forms of critical writing.

> Sooner or later, we learn, deconstruction turns on every critical reading or theoretical construction. When a decision is made, when authority emerges, when theory or criticism operates, then deconstruction questions. ... As soon as it does so, it becomes subversive. ... Ultimately, deconstruction effects revision of traditional thinking.

> To deconstruct a discourse is to show how it undermines the philosophy it asserts. ...

> A deconstruction, then, shows the text resolutely refusing to offer any privileged reading; ... deconstructive criticism clearly transgresses the limits established by traditional criticism.[28]

It is within the recent skirmishes between humanist and poststructuralist that this movement for the elimination of the traditional grounds of critical theory takes place, and from which Ellis's argument comes. What is called into question is the important issue of hierarchies of meaning and method. It is, it would seem from Ellis's question of contribution, that the need in humanistic studies for a certain kind of traditional hierarchy of meaning is necessary for the continuation of the *polis* or civil order upon which meaningfulness, as we know it, depends. In this instance, the self-evident status of the *polis* or civil grounds of meaningfulness are never severely interrogated; instead, it seems that the humanist, via Wittgenstein, shows an interest in maintaining the normalization of the range of meaning within the *polis* for meaningfulness. In this instance the word is an object which has a particular value in its difference from other words, and the value either naturally increases or naturally decreases depending on the eternality of the "civil" context or shared world. But what, then, is implicit within this understanding of "matters of human concern" as a mere language-game?

At least for humanists appropriating Wittgenstein, it seems as if language as an activity or form of life changes. In other words, there is a constant unfolding of the diversity of meaning within a continuous and harmonious civil context or shared world. The meaning within the shared world, civil, or public context takes on new meaning, but the civil or public remains

fixed, unerring, and unexamined as a conceptual construct and historical structure itself. Within this understanding of the sign, the word is abstracted and given objectivity as a game-piece on the surface of language itself. One has only to recall the Wittgensteinian chess-piece in order to understand the play of surfaces involved in this objectification. It is this objectivity which circulates within the system of exchange and either, according to Wittgensteinian humanists, maintains its newness or is superseded by another form of life – another meaning, another move. The objectification of the word, then, takes place on the unproblematized surface of the shared world. What allows this privileging of the public space is the philosophical tradition's investment in further mystifying meaning's connection to the world. Within this idealized paradigm articulated by the *notion* of shared world, the shared nature of the world itself is fixed and not produced by the free play of signification. Rather, meaning, for the Wittgensteinian humanist, is not the free play of signification upon a surface; instead, it exists within an idealized and ahistorical problematic set complementarily beside an Augustinian primordial presence in the word as object of contemplation. The move of the Wittgensteinian humanist, like his analytic cousins, is to turn from the world as a site of conflict and contestation into a harmonious shared or common surface, a natural phenomenon free from competing classes, or groups, or modes of intelligibility. The following passage delineates the limits of a contrary intellectual enterprise by pointing out that the work of philosophy consists in getting language to correspond to the reality of everyday life:

> It is the business of philosophy, not to resolve a contradiction by means of a mathematical or logico-mathematical discovery, but to make it possible for us to get a clear view of the state of mathematics that troubles us: the state of affairs before the contradiction is resolved. (And this

does not mean that one is sidestepping a difficulty.) [*Und damit geht man nicht etwa einer Schwierigkeit aus dem Wege.*]

The fundamental fact here is that we lay down rules, a technique, for a game, and that then when we follow the rules, things do not turn out as we had assumed. That we are therefore as it were entangled in our own rules [*Daß wir uns also gleichsam in unsern eigenen Regeln verfangen*].

This entanglement in our rules is what we want to understand (i.e. get a clear view of) [*Dieses Verfangen in unsern Regeln ist, was wir verstehen, d.h. übersehen wollen*].

It throws light on our concept of meaning something [*Es wirft ein Licht auf unsern Begriff des Meinens*]. For in those cases things turn out otherwise than we meant, had foreseen. That is what we say when, for example, a contradiction appears: "I didn't mean it like that" [*So hab' ich's nicht gemeint*].

The civil status of a contradiction, or its status in civil life: there is the philosophical problem [*Die bürgerliche Stellung des Widerspruchs, oder seine Stellung in der bürgerlichen Welt; das ist das philosophische Problem*].[29]

A humanist rereading of Wittgenstein's concept of rules sets up the conditions for mystifying the social context even further and eliding meaning production as a conflict of signs. At first, the rules, as they are delineated by Wittgenstein, allegedly draw attention away from any metaphysical/supernatural or self-evident origin of the meaning of a word. This is, perhaps, the intersubjectivity of Wittgensteinian and Derridean discourses, or philosophy as one continuous discourse since Plato. The civil (the *polis*), however, is the ahistorical, metaphysical (without cause) and acultural gameboard upon which the everyday meaning of

words is played out. For instance, a red apple, according to Wittgenstein, is a red apple, and a store clerk does not need a cosmic chart to decipher a red apple from a green apple. Instead of a metaphysical presence determining a word's meaning, Wittgensteinian humanists fetishize ordinary language by equating the mental image with the speech act.

The issue of deconstruction as a reading methodology is pertinent to the later Wittgensteinian language-game in that it provides a counter-reading to that of the humanists. This monitoring and establishing of knowledge, which the deconstructionist Wittgensteinian counters, takes place because the philosophical tradition has erected an impostor (the primordial presence in the object) from which it can only make lateral moves. Recent arguments, however, intertwining Wittgenstein with Derrida coalesce around the dismantling of the transcendental word-origin in an attempt to invigorate an acceptance of a plurality of (non)meaning within the rarefied everyday use of language and at the same time allow for the blocking of history. Henry Staten points to this "intertwining of threads of language"[30] which inevitably leads to a re-weaving of word-fibers. In other words, Wittgenstein deconstructs, in that his language folds in on itself through the exchange of word and mental image (context), causing decidability which becomes, through the vast play of surfaces, undecidability, in that decidability can now be only a metaphysical presupposition. Wittgenstein's word-fibers circulate within the vast system of exchange, and achieve meaningfulness in their "value" to the unproblematized public space. Staten describes this unstable state of language and of the word:

By twisting fibers together we get thread; by weaving threads together we get a text; by un-raveling the text into its threads and the threads into their fibers we get deconstruction, which is at the same time itself a fabric woven according to the variable pattern of the unweaving of the deconstructed fabric.[31]

The humanist's self-evidency of meaning within the word-in-public context, as we have seen, conveniently forgets the political economy of the sign and, at the same time, further naturalizes the overarching social structure by closely associating it with the naturalness or the Saussurean symbolic status of language. This move to naturalize various discourses is especially significant to the humanistic tradition's uncritical appropriation of Wittgenstein. The intersubjectivity, as Staten refers to it, is an instance of positing an anti-humanist understanding of language as a cultural production which is produced in relation to competing classes, or groups, or frames of intelligibility within the *polis*. It is still important to go beyond the immediate local focus of the word in the public context and proceed into the production of the *sign* and the sign system, and why this way of understanding the sign as a product of inclusions and eclipses of meaning within the *polis* threatens the ideological center of humanistic studies. Current humanist readings of Wittgenstein continue to elide this particular eclipsing condition in such a way as to reinstate confidence in certain sacred philosophical texts which continue to keep in place hierarchies of power and knowledge.

What is assumed in the humanist Wittgensteinian model is a unified subject which has a linguistic control over the production of meaning. Staten's Wittgenstein renders the subject in a quite different way:

46

The scene and every element of the scene before us swarm with accidental characters that threaten to squirm away in every direction – a Medusa's head alive with snakes that could get away. But are snakes really so horrifying? And suppose they did get away; suppose the scene before me, always threatening to get out of control now that the hardness of the law has been questioned, exploded into its characters and left me completely disoriented before apparent chaos and anarchy? "Then I should say something like 'I have gone mad'; *but that would merely be an expression of giving up the attempt to know my way about.*"[32]

The explosion of the hardness of the law to which Staten refers characterizes a Lyotardian postmodern condition as much as it does one of Wittgenstein and Derrida. With the stability of language now brought to crisis by poststructuralist thinkers, the humanistic paradigm becomes unmoored. Language within poststructuralist conceptual schemes does not take us back to the essence of humanity – an essence present in the world as such. The turn on Saussure's linguistic turn, and the subsequent turn on Wittgenstein's linguistic turn, render meaningless the traditional or paleo-humanist project. To return to Abrams's attack on the poststructuralist conceptual schemes is to re-evaluate language's role in constructing an aesthetic or a means of deciphering what is a matter of human concern. This evaluation, as it were, is a re-evaluation of an age or a report on knowledge.

The second prong of Abrams's attack is pointed at the aesthetic implications of poststructuralist thought. A poststructuralist conceptual scheme leads to a postmodern aesthetic which marks the inability of language to mean or to express the autonomy of the artist. What, then, is the postmodern? Jean-François Lyotard's *The Postmodern Condition: A Report on Knowledge* addresses a crisis in the way in which thought is structured at the end of the twentieth century. As Lyotard's sub-title indicates, knowledge is something that can be reported on as opposed to something that one has. Knowledge, thought, thinking, are connected to a larger discursive operation than the humanists – Abrams, for instance – have acknowledged. Lyotard's point is that thought at the end of the twentieth century is tied to the construction of grand narratives which celebrate and express the totality of the word, and which, in doing so, deny the existence and persistence of little narratives which do not order the world according to the categories of the grand narrative. A partial definition of "postmodern" would point to the notion that the postmodern actually comes before the modern – at that moment before modernism hardens its rules. The humanist paradigm requires that a subject be present in language and in art. It requires also that this subject is autonomous – free from the impositions of difference. A postmodern aesthetic runs contrary to the humanists' aesthetic, along at least two lines. First, there is not a moment of epistemological certitude and therefore no way of confirming a "concern" for the subject. Second, there is no longer a sacred to adjudicate a "concern."

47

CHAPTER 4

Disfiguring the sacred in art and religion

The sacred of the archaic world was not only the supreme value [*a valeur suprême*], not only the predominating value [*a valeur ordonnatrice*]: it stood for the whole realm of values [*Il était le domaine des valeurs*]. All that was unrelated to it was worthless and what pertained to it derived from it alone. It recognized no "heroes" other than its own.

(André Malraux, *The Metamorphosis of the Gods*)

PARASACRALITY

We find that our postmodern world bears little resemblance to the heroed archaic world described by André Malraux in *The Metamorphosis of the Gods*. It differs in that the postmodern world recognizes no heroes at all, let alone heroes who rise and fall in eternal conflicts. While it is a world bereft of or free from heroes, it is a world that is nevertheless still filled with conflict and struggle, but without the supreme value of the sacred to give those conflicts and struggles universal meaning and purpose. In the absence of a singular predominating value of the sacred, expressions of ultimacy can exist, according to Malraux in *The Voices of Silence*, only as a "third world" [*troisiéme monde]* which is located between "man's fleeting world [*le monde éphémère des hommes*] and the transcendent world of God [*le monde absolu de Dieu*]."[1] This liminal world, which is neither entirely fleeting nor entirely lasting, is the place of the divine; the place where ultimacy is inscribed, yet veiled. When one thinks of the liminal divine, one is, in effect, thinking theologically, attending to the seemingly inherent lack of completeness present in human existence. It is this lack, according to

Malraux, which gives rise to religious practice and artistic expression across the ages; it is a lack which folds back unto itself; a lack placed alongside, if not marked by, a hope to recuperate the loss or a hope to "commune with the Cosmos or the dark demonic powers of nature."[2] The folding back, doubling of the lack, deferring cosmos and chaos, posits human creative acts as losses; human creative acts, unlike the creative acts of the gods, exist in the shadows cast in the twilight. The artistic act and religious practice, both their performance and product, capture neither the brilliance of the Cosmos nor the darkness of demonic nature, but tenuously approximate both polarities; for Malraux, this is theological thinking in art.

Across the ages these approximations of the supreme sacred, both its brilliance and its darkness, have been understood as uniquely religious in nature, while also finding articulation in architecture, art, music, and literature. In a postmodern age, intimations and simulations of the sacred in art and religious life abound somewhat ironically in a world without a supreme sacred or singular ultimate concern. In the wake of the sacred in the archaic and modern world, postmodern life finds itself without immediate access to the supreme sacred. This irresolution is not merely the fragmented effect of modern life; for modern life is understood as the bifurcation of the world, one part sacred and the other part profane, with the two dialectically joined. The synthesis of fragments within the dialectic of the sacred and the profane sets the stage for a postmodern religious life which, much like the pressures Malraux faced, pressed Mircea Eliade to write prophetically in *Patterns in Comparative Religion* that

all the definitions given up till now of the religious phenomenon have one thing in common: each has its own way of showing that the sacred and the religious life are the opposite of the profane and the secular life. But as soon as you start to fix limits to the notion of the sacred you come upon difficulties – difficulties both theoretical and practical.[3]

This irony described by Eliade that we find so prevalent in our postmodern age can be understood, if we extend Eliade's thought, in terms of the peculiarity of a religious life without the dialectical synthesis of the world and heaven. As Eliade reflects, we are left with the unreconciled fragments of the divine and the world along with the question of how one moves beyond this opacity toward epiphany. The inability to fix the limits of the sacred and reveal its presence in human existence points to more than a mysterium that we must take on faith alone; it points also to a profound loss and the persistence of humankind's need to re-establish or render the sacred tangible in a postmodern age.

If we then return to the archaic world described by Malraux, we find a separation that is overcome by the power of the supreme value of the sacred. The ancient Egyptians, for instance, inscribed this overcoming when they fashioned terrestrial forms in conjunction with the underworld figures in an attempt to replace mere appearances with everlasting Truth. Unlike the Egyptians of the ancient past who created Maat to stand for that eternal Truth (light) contained within appearance, we find in a postmodern age that these difficulties in discerning Truth from appearances inevitably lead one into an epistemological, semantic, and ontological crisis that is characterized by the impossibility of reducing one reality to another. This would-be solution to the crisis, understood as a religious practice, privileges a totalized view of the sacred, the supreme sacred, over that of a heterological view of the para/sacred. It is this destabilization of ultimacy, brought on by the absence of either a transcendent sacred or a concrete profane, that defines our postmodern crisis. The work of the ancient stone-

carver or architect is not that much different from that of the postmodern writer who, too, fashions terrestrial-like forms. Unlike the ancient fashioner of signs, however, the postmodern fashioner of signs works without the template of a universal sacred. Rendering an image or marking a surface in a meaningful way, writing, is a continuation of an ancient struggle of the human condition, finitude, and mortality. The parasacred's place on the limits or margins of sacrality calls upon us today to ask the questions: How do we address our own finitude, our own mortality in the absence of the supreme ultimate? Where do we, or can we, find expressions of the sacred in postmodern existence? What does it mean to think religiously in the absence of the ultimate?

SACRED COMMUNITY

These questions direct us toward those instances in which the gap between the sacred and the profane seems, at first glance, to be bridged. As an example of this bridging, the relationship one finds taking shape between the past, present, and future in the ideological work of the 1893 Columbian Exposition presents the very theoretical and practical "difficulties" Eliade refers to in *Patterns in Comparative Religion*. Greek and Egyptian revivalism suggest a crisis in constructing a genealogy of America. In other words, which origin comes first? Does America begin in Egypt? Africa? Or, does America begin with and end the first white civilization in Athens? These crises are understood as rupturings of continuity and the available plane of representation. These ruptures and the ensuing recognition that the sacred is not limited and wholly representable in the profane create a possibility for an expression of exteriority and another, alternative, sacrality and genesis: "But it is quite certain that anything man has ever handled, felt, come in contact with or loved *can* become a hierophany."[4] The desire at the Columbian Exposition, as we saw earlier, is for a hierophany or dialectical moment which would end the crisis of origin and, at the same time, bring a moment that might gather together a differentiated and hierarchical sacred and profane world (thereby filling the newly opened space with a supreme sacred). Clearly this particular crisis was not addressed, and the Columbian Exposition lacked a necessary reconciling absolute exteriority. The sacred in its work to contain everything cannot serve the dual function as its own interior and absolute exterior.

A response to the sacred's inability to contain itself within itself, and the absence of an absolute exteriority, take shape in reconfiguring the sacred as heterogeneous; the sacred, as it is understood as an absolute reality which transcends the world, becomes more accessible when conceptualized as a limit or boundary rather than as an ultra-determining reality. As a limit-concept and not as a reality, the parasacred, I will argue, offers an approximation of ultimacy through a process of negation. This displacement or negation is in contrast to a definition of sacrality through a process of identification. Here one needs to engage with the difficulties of constructing an approximated ultimacy or, better put, an ultimacy of approximation along with an alternative methodology or a polymethodic inquiry which, unlike the prior methodologies given to date, avoids, according to Eliade, a reinstantiation of a transcendent "absolute":

It is unlikely that there is any animal or any important species of plant in the world that has

53

never had a place in religion. In the same way too, every trade, art, industry and technical skill either began as something holy, or has, over the years, been invested with religious value. This list could be carried on to include man's everyday movements (getting up, walking, running), his various employments (hunting, fishing, agriculture), all his physiological activities (nutrition, sexual life, etc.); perhaps too the essential words of the language, and so on … it seems improbable that there remains anything that has not at some time been so transfigured.[5]

A necessary consideration in engaging this need for an approximation of ultimacy and an alternative methodology which can account for the subtle disfigurations of the ordinary includes a tempering of methodology with epiphany. In other words, this "tempering" of methodology can be understood as an insistence on understanding a discursive practice in relation to an external point outside a given discursive frame which cannot be circumscribed or written as anything other than an exteriority or excess. This amounts to an infinite framing of the discursive frame(s). Doubling the frame or multiplying the frame sets into motion an infinite positing of an exteriority, as well as an approximated ultimacy. Ultimacy drifts and is pressed up against yet another threshold. To better see the metamorphosis of the sacred in relation to shifting understandings of the ultimate, it is necessary to compare and study its emergence, metamorphosis, and persistence in three areas of text production: religious painting, a religious life, and the discipline of religion. In all three instances, the issue of the frame or the discursive enclosure illuminates the darkened aspects of the interior and, in so doing, creates a shift in the frame as well as a shift from darkness to brilliance and brilliance to darkness. It is this disfiguration which I understand as, and will explain in terms of, the process of parasacralization.

Theological thinking in painting is different from religious painting, in that theological thinking denotes the posing of the *question* of ultimacy while "religious painting" is religious in terms of its content, images, and themes. Perhaps a useful instance of theological thinking in painting, multiple frames, and drifting ultimacy, can be found in an art-historical context described by André Malraux. In *The Metamorphosis of the Gods*, Malraux puts forward the argument that civilization evolves in relation to shifting absolutes. He expresses this shift in what is defined as the ultimate as a struggle against mortality; an attempt made by humankind to penetrate eternity:

> We sense the existence of that world, but do not know its nature. We are aware of it as one is made aware of the presence of a huge, frameless mirror by the images reflected in it [*d'un immense miroir sans bords par les images qu'il nous présenterait*]. We are beginning to see that the West discovered that world at the same time as it discovered the world of history, and that these two entities, akin yet adverse, have been haunting it ever since the creation of figures inspired by Faith, by the unreal or by an ideal of beauty, ceased as a result of their joint influence; ever since a sequence of philosophies, voicing that "sense of time" [*sentiment du temps*] which seems to be an obsession which our present age, bereft of Eternity, has taught us to see in Time man's chief antagonist [*dans le sentiment de l'éternal, a fait du temps l'interlocuteur capital de l'homme*].[6]

54

Set alongside the ancient problem of recovering Truth from appearances, Malraux examines a series of Jan Van Eyck's (1390–1441) paintings which also marks this shift in absolutes from the sacred to the secular. The paintings demonstrate a turn away from the supernatural sacred in art, and in painting in particular, toward the ordinary secular, which is in crisis. For Malraux, Van Eyck's paintings refigure the subject of painting; however, more importantly, Van Eyck tampers with the frame, questions what is presented as sacred and what is ultimate. Whereas the subject in a mosaic, for instance, would ordinarily focus his or her eyes on the divine presence, Van Eyck's subject focuses on the painter artist. *The Goldsmith Jan de Leeuw* (1436) and the altarpiece *Adoration of the Lamb* (1432) represent what Malraux describes as the gradual desacralization of art, and what I understand as the parasacralization of art. *Adoration of the Lamb*, painted by Jan Van Eyck with the assistance of his brother Hubert, is on the threshold of the absolute in that it refigures the frame(s) of painting. While the work is devotional, and is clearly in the service of the sacred as it was understood at the time, it nevertheless begins to upset the construction of sacrality itself. The altarpiece, in the form of a multipanel polyptych, simulates the Bible, as its panels open and close like a book. Its theme, the union of God and humanity, represents the Trinitarian nature of God in conjunction with (from top left to right) Adam, a choir of angels, Mary, Jesus (with a triple tiara), John the Baptist, angels playing the harp, and Eve (above her, Cain slaying Abel). Below these we see the lamb on the altar, the Fountain of Living Waters, and, in the corners, the faithful descending upon the altar. Van Eyck's altarpiece is at first glance a pious work proclaiming Christian aspirations. The twenty panels representing the New Jerusalem had a number of frames which enclose each scene; the first "frame" is Christ; the second "frame" is the Cathedral of St Bavo in Ghent; the third "frame" is the artists' faith; and the fourth "frame" is the actual frame of the panels, the Gothic tabernacle that enclosed them. Hubert's framework, or working of the frame, was unfortunately destroyed during the religious strife of the latter part of the sixteenth century, leaving us to speculate on its significance. If one were to apply Malraux's argument to the history of the *Adoration of the Lamb*, the notion of a shifting absolute becomes quite clear, in the sense that each frame or framing moment has, in the course of history, been broken and replaced both literally and figuratively. The Ghent altarpiece undergoes its own metamorphosis, in that the panel remained closed throughout the year except on feast days when they were unfolded. Malraux suggests that this was an attempt to bypass the divine, the third world, and directly experience the sacred:

> Like the cathedral portals, Giotto's frescos had been *permanent* manifestations of Christian faith. But the Ghent Altarpiece displayed its *Adoration* and *Angels* only when the wings were opened on great feast days and, once the festival was over, it closed them on this noble celebration of the spirit of the Crusades. Thus these fleeting disclosures had, for the congregation, the effect of sudden revelations and quickened feelings differing from those aroused by familiar portal statues, scenes on tympana and even the Italian fresco. Van Eyck was not admired *more* than Giotto, but for other reasons; the admiration he inspired came not only from his power of expressing the divine by means of appearance, but also from his introduction of appearance into a world that sublimated it [*l'apparence dans un monde qui la métamorphose*] and was other than that in which St Joseph seemed a simple carpenter. It was a world in which a carpenter could become St Joseph and Chancellor Rolin meet the Virgin. Far from accepting the supremacy of Nature, he exercised his power of bending appearance to his will and using it to express what

55

> had hitherto been kept apart from it [*Loin de découvrir le primat de la nature, il découvre son propre d'exprimer par la complaisante apparence ce qui était jusque-là séparé d'elle*].[7]

The fleeting disclosures, as Malraux describes them, were disclosures of the sacred in the world. In other words, Van Eyck's Ghent altarpiece, unlike the frescoes of Giotto, *Miracle of the Spring* (c.1296), *Pieta* (1305–6), and *St Francis Renouncing His Father* (c.1296–1300), represented the sacred as the actually real, without mediation. In this sense, the "actually real" has been (mis)understood as the desacralization of art. It seems, rather, that the "actually real" points more to the sacrality surrounding and transfiguring the ordinary or real world than the actual eradication of it. Van Eyck's paintings are, in this sense, religious in both content and thought. Van Eyck raised the issue of sacrality and ultimacy in a way in which it had never been raised before.

The same understanding of desacralization continues in Malraux's reading of Baroque art. In the Baroque era, Caravaggio's (1571–1610) work is thought by Malraux to represent a further separation of the sacred from the profane. His painting *The Conversion of Paul* (c.1601) was criticized for depicting a biblical figure as a common person. The adaptation of Paul's (Saul's) conversion to Christianity by Caravaggio emphasized the ordinary nature of the calling – he fell from his horse. Perhaps the most "sacrilegious" of Caravaggio's work is *Death of a Virgin*, in which a drowned corpse represents the Madonna. While Italian Baroque art was primarily in the service of the Catholic popes who used grandiose art to document the triumph after the Counter-Reformation, Caravaggio's desacralization of art, as Malraux calls it, uncovered what I refer to as the parasacred element in painting. *The Calling of St Matthew* and *Supper at Emmaus* depict biblical figures as common people in a common setting replete with pubs, dandies, and wormy fruit. Caravaggio's *Il tenebroso* not only describes his use of shadowy background: it points to a silent brilliance. As art historians would have it, Caravaggio extends theological thinking in painting by refiguring or, in this case, disfiguring the divine, the relationship between a transcendent order and the world. It is this refiguration or disfiguration which Jacques Derrida, in *Memoirs of the Blind: The Self-Portrait and Other Ruins*, notices as the absence of light (sight) or of the allusion to light in the painting which gives it its force. In other words, the shadowiness of the painting *Il tenebroso* is possible through the incomplete or impossible negation of light, the absolute. Here, like Van Eyck, Caravaggio does not so much desacralize as parasacralize painting:

> Each time a divine punishment is cast down upon sight in order to signify the mystery of election, the blind become witnesses to the faith. An inner conversion at first seems to transfigure light itself. Conversion of the inside, conversation on the inside: in order to enlighten the spiritual sky on the inside, the divine light creates darkness in the earthly sky on the outside. This veil between two lights is the experience of bedazzlement, the very bedazzlement that, for example, knocks Paul to the ground on the road to Damascus. A conversion of the light literally bowls him over. Oftentimes his horse is also thrown violently to the ground, bowled over or knocked to the ground in the same fall, its eyes sometimes turned like its master's toward a blinding source of light or the divine word. In Caravaggio's painting (Rome, Santa Maria del Popolo) only the horse remains standing. Lying outstretched on the ground, eyes closed, arms open and reaching up toward the sky, Paul is turned toward the light that bowled him over. The brightness seems to fall upon him as if it were reflected by the animal itself.[8]

56

The sacred in painting cannot merely vanish from content or thought. Instead, it remains present through its "absence" or its suppression. The darkness of Caravaggio's painting makes sense only in light of the absence of light. It is the eclipsing of the sacred by the world which produces its power in painting. The sacred cannot be eliminated altogether; it must, instead, be transformed, transfigured, or disfigured, relegated to the edges of the surface or subsumed in the images.

Just as painting in the thirteenth, fourteenth, and fifteenth centuries can be generally understood to reflect, as it were, the power of belief among the ordinary, painting in the sixteenth and seventeenth centuries reflected the power of institutions, the re-invigorated Church, an emerging aristocracy, the expansion of the bourgeois merchant class, and the rise of scientific knowledge. Just as Van Eyck's and Caravaggio's paintings marked a shift in the history of absolutes from the supernaturally sacred to the ordinarily sacred, the parasacred, Diego Velazquez's *Las Meninas* (1656) indicates yet another shift in ultimacy and sacrality. While the overt allusion to religion or religious figures is altogether absent in Velazquez's painting, religious thinking is not. In the works of Van Eyck and Caravaggio, religious images and symbols initiated religious thinking. Velazquez, on the other hand, thinks religiously in the sense that he thinks the limit of painting is pure or contentless exteriority. Foucault, in *The Order of Things: An Archaeology of the Human Sciences*, writes:

> The painter is looking, his face turned slightly and his head leaning towards one shoulder. He is staring at a point to which, even though it is invisible, we, the spectators, can easily assign an object, since it is we, ourselves, who are that point: our bodies, our faces, our eyes. The spectacle he is observing is thus doubly invisible: first, because it is not represented within the

space of the painting, and, second, because it is situated precisely in that blind point, in that essential hiding-place into which our gaze disappears from ourselves at the moment of our actual looking. And, yet, how could we fail to see that invisibility, there in front of our eyes, since it has its own perceptible equivalent, its sealed-in figure, in the painting itself?[9]

Foucault's reading of the painting shares a concern about the limitless nature of the "sacred" with Eliade's understanding of the sacred–profane dialectic. This shared concern can to some extent be characterized as the notion that sacrality, ultimacy, or meaning reside at the edges of a text, as well as in the center. Both Foucault and Eliade, although approaching the issue with much different intellectual agendas, come to a shared understanding: an epiphany for Foucault and a hierophany for Eliade. Foucault shares with the reader his laughter out of which *The Order of Things* was born. What struck Foucault as humorous was the mutability of distinguishing between the Same and the Other. The Chinese encyclopedia[10] described in Borges's text "shattered ... all the familiar landmarks of my thought – *our* thought – breaking up all the ordered surfaces and all the planes with which we are accustomed to tame the wild profusion of existing things, and continuing long afterwards to disturb and threaten with collapse our age-old distinction between the Same and the Other." One can easily understand this laughter as an epiphany – an acute awareness of the exterior and the lack of completeness of any given discursive frame, Malraux's metamorphosis. More specifically, epiphanies such as the one described by Foucault rupture both theoretical discursive frames and practical planes of reference by pointing out either a contradiction in a logic chain – semblable things dissemble – or, in the case of Mircea Eliade's work, a hierophany that marks the dissimulation of the sacred in transfiguration of the ordinariness in life: "in every

religious frame-work there have always been profane beings and things beside the sacred."[11] Foucault's laughter carries with it a moment of solace in so far as the internal integrity of a discursive frame is shattered. For Foucault, it is the laughter, the epiphany, that shatters the age-old distinctions between the Same and the Other. It is this moment, I will argue, that allows us to look more carefully at the complexity of the sacred. What becomes visible, in the same sense that visibility is constructed in *Las Meninas*, is the invisibility of the parasacred. Foucault's laughter opens the sacred and Eliade's hierophany to the infinite process of doubling the frame. Fixing the limits of the sacred and then watching those limits wash away is, contrary to the conventional reading of Eliade, very much a part of theological thinking. If we consider Foucault's reading of Velazquez's painting *Las Meninas* to work as a preface to reading Eliade's approximation of the sacred, we find that the age-old distinction between the sacred and the profane collapses.

The dual questions, implied in Eliade's writings, of the loss and what is the sacred are further complicated by Foucault's re-articulation of the *mise en abyme*. Formalists have considered the *mise en abyme* to be a tool of criticism and, as David Carroll points out in *Paraesthetics: Foucault, Lyotard, and Derrida*,[12] this often has led to a suppression of the exterior in the name of aesthetic closure. Foucault, on the other hand, finds that *Las Meninas* invites an exterior which places the abyss not so much within as outside of the frame. With Foucault's reading of *Las Meninas*, we are left with two reflections: aesthetic and historical. In the first, the aesthetic, we see that formalist interpretive strategies exclude the notion of doubling the frame and thereby construct a text as autonomous, self-enclosed. In the second, the historical, we see this aesthetic proposition disturbed. Foucault's reading finds that Velazquez's painting represents *representation*. In other words, as Foucault indicates, the painting betrays the aesthetic rule of self-enclosure. The episteme governing painting in the Classical age had, as evidenced by *Las Meninas*, an alternative episteme which disturbed the established rules of representation and thought. Foucault then directs our attention to thinking, or theological thinking. As a spectator, we know that we are not the image in the mirror. We are other than that image and yet we stand in that place. In other words, the image in the mirror reflects another exterior which we must take into consideration:

> Space is turned inside out, and the category of all categories or the space of all spaces is empty at its core, impossible inasmuch as it is all-encompassing. The ground in which it could be rooted is undercut through the very process of self-inclusiveness. This paradox, and the instability it produces, fascinate the archaeologist of *The Order of Things* – an archaeologist looking for any sign that the ultimate foundation of order is not in itself or any metaprinciple, but the instability or disorder inherent in all order.[13]

Foucault argues via *Las Meninas* that the outside is multiform and, as a result, empty of transcendent character. This has severe consequences for those embarking on an archaeology of the sacred with the expectation of hearing or recording the secret of the Sphinx. The epiphany marked by laughter which shatters the age-old distinction between the Same and the Other has a relevance to the age-old distinction between the sacred and the profane. The theory of semblance gives way to dissemblance as the parasacred makes itself "visible" and thereby offers an alternative and vanishing ultimacy that "grounds" the human mode of being.

58

DISFIGURING THE DISCIPLINE

Art leads us into the history of religion through the impossibility of representing the ultimate, the sacred. We have seen, through the insights of Malraux and Foucault, as well as of Eliade, the metamorphosis or disfigurement of painting as it attempts to render intelligible the dialectic of the sacred and profane. One could ask if the same metamorphosis or disfigurement take places within religious studies, as it, too, attempts to make intelligible the ultimate, the sacred. I believe that there is a strong parallel, and, to establish this point more completely, the "beginnings" of the history of religion must be looked at carefully through the work of Mircea Eliade, a figure whose work brings into conversation art, literature, and religion.

Historians of religion and scholars in the humanities who are interested in pursuing this dialectic of the sacred via Eliade's work find that autobiography infiltrates scholarship in unusual ways. In attempting to grasp the range and magnitude of Eliade's work, scholars have centralized one or two "dominant" concepts (the sacred–profane dialectic and morphology) and have built quite an elaborate explanatory structure attempting to encompass and explicate his thought. Eliade's writings, however, proved then – and continue to prove to this day – not to be easily set to rest or circumscribed within the conventional discourses of the academy; simply the task of reading the vastness of his oeuvre (in Romanian, French, and English) is in itself forbidding. In addition to that daunting obstacle, one finds, through careful reading of his writings, that the many turns and folds of Eliade's thought, in his scholarly and creative work, strongly resist the circumscription, structuration, and totalization which are so much a part of scholarship today. As one begins to read further through Eliade's oeuvre (both the scholarly texts and his *litterature fantastique*), a profound sense of the presence–absence of a remainder or an excess which stands outside of the realm of academic discourse and of intelligibility itself is encountered. This does not mean that Eliade's methodology is, as some have argued in the past, irresponsible – that he did not (as if he should) systematically fit things together. Nor does it mean necessarily that Eliade was a mystic or a Christian by default. It does mean, however, that Eliade's thinking, his methodology, as it were, was dynamic and to a greater extent performative in its (creative) hermeneutic; his ruminations over the sacred never reached closure because he strongly felt that the sacred (power and ultimacy) continues to disrupt events within the profane, time and history.

This sense of the remainder, the darkness after the brilliance, the excessive condition of the sacred or the inability to exhaust the modalities of the sacred, in human existence comes to light in Eliade's artistic and scholarly endeavors in the language of a quest, a quest complete with all the accompanying romantic images the word implies: it is a bringing together of the ultimate and humankind. Of course, in the case of Eliade, the line between the artistic and the scholarly is finely drawn – so finely drawn, I'll add, that one often has the sense that Eliade's creative writing is seducing the reader into the realm of the scholarly and that the scholarly is seducing one into the realm of creative writing: "That which characterizes us as human and defines us *vis-à-vis* other orders of nature and God ... is the instinct for transcendence, the craving to be free from oneself and to pass over into the other, the urgent need to break the iron band of individuality."[14] No other concept more brings to mind, troubles, and defines for scholars the philosophy of Mircea Eliade than "the sacred." No other of Eliade's central concepts figures so prominently and ambiguously in the whole of

his work; at the same time, no other concept has been given over to such varying interpretations – often offered by Eliade himself. What has become in recent years a sizable body of work founded on a delimited range of definitions of the sacred and on how Eliade's notion of the sacred, similar to Michel Foucault's "wrinkle, amounts to an intellectual wager rather than a comprehensive definition": Does not the sacred, in all of its appearances, represent a struggle to overcome an indefatigable antagonism? An attempt to know ourselves through the Other; a futile attempt to close a gap or straighten a fold, a separation from ourselves, the Other, and God? For Eliade, although he constantly recasts and refines this separation throughout his scholarly and creative work, it is the "craving" or the unfailing *desire* to complete ourselves rather than the actual act of completion itself which moves the quest. Who we are, for Eliade, comes to expression in that space of "desiring" as it is experienced through the tension arising between becoming and being. In "Literature and Fantasy," the Foreword to two novellas *Les Trois Graces* and *With the Gypsy Girls* Eliade makes bold claims on behalf of the artistic act's power to address and engage this antagonism – an antagonism which constitutes for Eliade a tragic fate:

> The tragic fate, which only a few realize in all its depths, of not being able to go out of yourself except by losing yourself, of not being able to communicate soul to soul (because any communication is illusory, except for love, which is a communion), of remaining terrified and alone in a world which in appearance is osmotic, so intimate – that tragic fate can only incite an unwearying struggle against itself, an immensely varied combat in opposition to laws. Hence the magical, artistic impulse of genius which cries that the law is for others, while play and fantasy are for the demon in us, for the artist and the dreamer. We are conditioned by creation

and are ourselves created. But that creative and self-revealing instinct transcends creation. We create through play, and we realize that the dimension of dream wherein we enjoy absolute freedom, where categories of existence are ignored and fate surpressed. Any revolt against the laws of fate must have the character of play, of the divine.[15]

It is, one can imagine Eliade saying, the possibility of artistic play in and around the separation from and loss of ourselves and the Other that gives rise to our collective humanity. Eliade continues this emphasis on the unifying potential of artistic play by asserting that it is only through artistic play that humanity can initiate the "beginning of a new world." Eliade is careful here, more careful than some of his readers have been over the years, to accentuate the instability of artistic play – its dangerously spontaneous and performative nature. Artistic play, as Eliade describes it, cannot be categorized or written into enforceable rules or laws. On the contrary, artistic play, as it corresponds to Eliade's concept of the sacred, is without rule and law: it is part of the divine: "It matters little that this world will find its own new laws quickly, laws over which new others will be unable to pass. It remains a magical, demiurgical creation, just as a work of art even if completed, it falls under physical, social, economic, or artistic laws."[16] The role of the sacred in the artistic act, then, is not an aesthetic or prescriptive one. Instead, the sacred is the condition for the possibility of the artistic act: it is the differential play that occurs between eternity and finitude. Without the sacred – that other plane of reference which threatens to rupture the plane of the profane by continually standing, in a menacing way, outside of intelligible categories – artistic play would be subjugated to a rule, whether aesthetic, political, economic, or ideological. Artistic play left merely to be understood in terms of available categories, for Eliade, denies that

fundamental human experience of "craving" the self and the Other. Here, artistic play and Eliade's new humanism come together through the concept of the quest in such a way as to open the world to new ways of understanding. If we understand the antagonism between becoming and being as an invitation to undertake a journey or quest, then the world, with all of its possible answers known and unknown, opens onto infinity. This can be understood as the path of new humanism. Perhaps it is the sacred, understood as the condition for the possibility of the artistic act and, for that matter, of human existence, that can best explain the nature of the quest by way of Eliade's unique status as both an artist and a scholar.

As an artist, a novelist, and as a scholar, an historian of religion, Eliade bridged the two arenas with his understanding of the creative act. As a novelist he asked seemingly obvious or fundamental questions, such as why things are the way they are. In *Les Trois Graces*, Eliade examines cell morphology and cancer-cell metastasis by way of alchemy and folklore and, as a result, embarks on a questioning of "change" – the changing morphology of the sacred and its historical manifestations. He calls upon the discourses of alchemy and folklore again when he gives the history of humanism by way of Hermes Trismegistus in his *Encyclopedia of Religious Ideas*. In this instance, Hermes Trismegistus and the *Corpus hermeticum* (a text translated from the Greek by Marsillo Ficino at the behest of Cosimo de'Medici prior to his translation of the *Dialogues*) represent an often undervalued anterior moment in the rise of Italian Renaissance humanism. Eliade's creative and scholarly works offer something that the general history of Western thought often overlooks – the philosophical and cultural significance of changing structures as they are marked by the often suppressed modes of magic and alchemy in the Western tradition. References to Hermeticism in Eliade's work are not merely interesting footnotes to history: they are challenges to the way things in the world are ordered; they are disfigurations of the ordinary and unfoldings of the sacred in history.

If the artistic act is understood as the desire to disfigure/transcend oneself, whether in art or scholarship, by participating in the unfolding of the sacred within history *through ecstatic experience*, then Eliade's autobiography (which is as much a literary achievement as a chronicle of a life) provides the material necessary to study the complexity of Eliade's concepts of the sacred and of art as they come together in this instance of the dis/transfiguration of the ordinary. Contrary to what many think of Eliade's work, and within it of the dis/transfiguration of the ordinary, he was not pointing in the direction of an autonomous transcendental plane which infuses things in the world with a degree of meaning; he was not articulating a negative theology; nor was he articulating a mimetic theory of art. At best, one could say that he was ambiguous about the nature of any higher reality, about which he made it a point to remain as vague as possible. His *Autobiography Vol. 1, Journey East, Journey West, 1907–1937*, and *Vol. 2, Exile's Odyssey, 1937–1960*, serve simultaneously to clarify and confuse many of Eliade's central themes as they relate to how the ordinary undergoes this transfiguration and participates in an alternative ordering. This leaves the remaining twenty-six years of his life to his published journal and diary *No Souvenirs*. The theme of the autobiography itself can be understood in terms of transfiguration and rearrangement. The dust-jacket to Volume 1 has a photograph of Eliade as a young man in India, while Volume 2 depicts an older and more contemplative Eliade. The autobiography begins and ends with a dis/transfiguration of Eliade's identity. He begins Volume 1 by describing the curious circumstances of his name. He tells the reader that his father Gheorghe Ieremia changed his name to Eliade for the reason that Gheorghe Ieremia

greatly admired the works of the Romanian writer Eliade-Radulescu. There is more to this story than a name-change, and Eliade layers on top of that name-change a separation from both family and place. The name change, in effect, restructured his connection to the extended family and placed the Eliades at a distance from both family and ethnic relations.[17] Eliade viewed this name-change symbolically, using it to express a persistent fluidity in his identity throughout his life. After a fire in the Meadville-Lombard School of Religion destroyed many of his papers, Eliade, just before his death, resigned himself to life's ironies, accepting the conflagration as yet another instance of his transformation.

Within the theme of dis/transfiguration, the autobiography marks the intersection of two arcs. The first is Eliade's life, his personal epiphanies, and the second his methodology. One may find it odd in the case of Eliade to draw a distinction between the two: life and methodology. This, however, is not so odd when one reads, time and again, Eliade describing the craving for epiphantic moments within the ordinariness of life. In "Earliest Recollections" from Volume 1, Eliade conveys to the reader the intensity of the "craving" for transcendence in early childhood, and it is alongside these first memories that Eliade expresses the point of contact between his life and his methodology. His childhood experience of entering the "forbidden" room in the house where he lived left him transfixed with emotion aroused by the encounter with taboo. The room, as Eliade recalls it, was pervaded by an "eerie iridescent light." The transfiguration of the ordinary[18] room into a "fairy-tale" place stands to illustrate Eliade's deep passion, even as a child, for forbidden places:

> I would relive with the same intensity the moment when I had stumbled into that paradise of incomparable light. I practiced for many years this exercise of recapturing the epiphantic

moment, and I would find again the same plenitude. I would slip into it as into a fragment of time devoid of duration – without beginning and without end.[19]

This early childhood experience does more than illustrate a curiosity about "forbidden places." It conveys Eliade's own sense of the importance of the dis/transfiguration of the ordinary in both local hierophanies (non-generalizeable within history) and mythico-symbolic hierophanies (generalizeable within history). He does not abandon this epiphantic moment to the dreams of childhood. Instead, Eliade continues to value the intensity of the experience in his adult life. And, much more than that I maintain, he carries it with him throughout his years, drawing on that intensity and using it as a cornerstone of his methodology and, by implication, his vision for a new discipline (history of religion) and as an integral part of coming to understand the complexity of the human mode of existence (new humanism).

The apparent separation of experience from the understanding of that particular experience takes many forms in Eliade's thought. In this case, the separation presses on two areas which are interdependent. First, and most direct, is the personal experience of the sacred as Eliade marks it in his autobiography in terms of epiphany. Second and, as some may argue, less direct, is the over-arching historical framework for understanding the epiphanic moment.

Eliade's history of religion and his new humanism call into question the definitions and categories which render the personal epiphanic moment intelligible. This division is an anterior moment to Eliade's methodology and takes the form of positivism over and against phenomenology, with Eliade's hermeneutics eventually moderating the two. One of the questions to arise in the scientific study of religion concerns what are to count as the data.

The answer to the question had consistently excluded the religious data of the non-Western ("primitive") world. Unlike the scientific study of religion, phenomenology included the religious data of the "primitive," and asked how the data are to be understood. Or, as Rudolf Otto asked: "What constitutes experience?" In *The History of Religions: Understanding Human Experience*, Joseph Kitagawa details an evolution of religious thought in the North American academy culminating in Eliade's vision of a new discipline, the history of religion. Although, as Kitagawa explains, comparative studies in religions were becoming common in the later nineteenth century, it seems clear that it was not until the end of the Second World War that the "Euro-centric dreams" ended.

THE SUBJECT OF A DISCIPLINE

The brief history of Eliade's thought recounted here clarifies a crucial issue in the development of an understanding of what it means to think religiously. In a sense, the issue comes down to methodology, or the tension between verification and falsification. A methodology should, as many would argue, provide a means of collecting data and of verifying or falsifying conclusions drawn from those data. Collection seems to be easy enough, except when one asks "What *should* I be collecting?" Eliade's methodology, if one were to call it that, does not provide a means of verification or falsification in the conventional sense. Eliade's methodology is not a methodology at all, because when asked how he came to understand or interpret some datum he would confess to having only looked at it and to see just what he could see. His understanding of a text or ritual was existential. Statements to that effect led many to see Eliade as a mystic who came intuitively to his conclusions. The issue of methodology, I will argue, is more complicated. Eliade's "methodology" does not work within the restrictions of verification and falsification. Instead, it works around those restrictions. Verification and falsification, for Eliade, are not part of objective reality, but are experiences of the world and experiences of the sacred. These experiences are hermeneutical experiences conditioned by a non-specific sacred. Experience, then, is a derivative of that sacred. It is the sacred that presents the supreme value from which things are ordered. An experience of the sacred, a hierophany, is a transfiguration of the order, the world. A hierophantic moment is one in which two experiences are held contradictorily, equally and simultaneously: the rain is a condensation of water vapor/the rain is from the gods. As Eliade indicates, everything in the world has, at one time, been part of the sacred – that is to say, held to mean two different things equally and simultaneously. For instance, a dream is both an imaging act and a communication. The two distinct meanings do not form a dialectic yielding a combined-thing, but rather mark a fissure in the surface *and* depth of knowledge. Eliade's "methodology" is an anti-methodology in so far as it displaces the epistemological grounds for verification–falsification.

Theological thinking in religion is the recognition of a divide, not only between perception and understanding, but between being and the world. This divide, an unbridgeable divide, is expressed through oppositions found in configuring the world. Eliade notes the end of the Euro-centric dream and its turn toward and away from waking. In a sense, the dream's end begins, for Eliade, a new form of knowledge which supersedes the prior form. This "new form" of knowledge in the West shares its appearance with the untotalizable Other contained within history. If one were to continue the metaphor of the wrinkle or fold, Max Muller's introduction

of the *Rig Veda* into the study of religion would represent that instance in which the fabric of knowledge is interrupted by an experience of the sacred. The *Rig Veda* offered for the West another spiritual source, another god(s), but more importantly, it seems, offered another sacrality and humanity.

The paradigmatic shifts within the study of religion(s) can be described as beginning with the scientific study of religion (*religio naturalis*), as it was defined by such scholars as Max Muller, E.B. Tylor, R.R. Marrett, Andrew Lang, and Wilhelm Schimdt, with its dependence on Enlightenment thinking, evolutionary theory and the preoccupation with recovering the essence of humankind's common religious heritage. *Religio naturalis* sought to reveal the essence of religion or the absolute truth of religious belief (Christianity) through the philological study of Indo-European languages. The stable structure of language, it was felt, could provide the way and the means to uncovering essential truth, and give to the West that which was "lost."

Religio naturalis and the stability of language underwent modification and elaboration by the phenomenologists of religion (Rudolf Otto and Gerardus van der Leeuw) who first dismissed the notion of the inferiority of the "primitive religious experience" and sought to connect that experience to the religious experience of the modern by way of stabilizing the human subject in the world. Since language no longer provided the exclusive path to understanding religious experience, religious data required a bracketing (the epoche) before one had the eidetic vision. Van der Leeuw in particular understood that phenomenological experience and understanding were exclusively human attributes. Since all human beings have these capabilities, then, van der Leuuw postulated, all aspects of human life across time and culture must resonate with these characteristics; the object and the subject reciprocate in the form of worship. In this sense, the eidetic vision is the consequence of five stages of inquiry:

> Van der Leeuw proposes a five step hermeneutical procedure. First, "what has become manifest," that is, the phenomenon, must be given a name (e.g. sacrifice, sacrament, service, worship, etc.). Second, we must "interpolate" the phenomenon into our own lives, because reality is always "*my* reality, history *my* history." Third, we must apply the principle of *epoche* and thus, in following these procedures, we find that "the chaotic and obstinate 'reality' thus becomes a manifestation, a revelation. The empirical, ontal, or metaphysical *fact* becomes datum; the object, living speech; rigidity, expression." While van der Leeuw affirms the formula of *Geistewissenschaften*, namely, "experience, expression, and understanding," he reminds us that "the intangible experience in itself cannot be apprehended nor mastered, but that it manifests something to us, an appearance."[20]

Could Western civilization use the Other as a guide to spiritual fulfillment? In the post-Great War era, phenomenologists of religion began incorporating lessons learned from sociology, anthropology, and psychology to fulfill that quest and set the framework for understanding religious experience. *Religionwissenschaften* broadened the scope of limited comparative studies in religions by extending, systematically, the discipline into the myths, symbols, and rituals of humankind's religious life. These historical data, it was felt, contained within them humankind's collective religious heritage and the hope for Western spirituality.

The search for humankind's collective religious heritage necessitated the construction of a bridge connecting universal human history and individual history, a melting and blending of

historical horizons. Dilthey writes in *Hermeneutics and the Study of History*: "Hermeneutics is the rise of the individual to the knowledge of the universal history, the universalization of the individual" (p. 122). What produces the universalization of the individual is a common humanity revealed through archetypal meanings and the consistency of a humanity across time and culture. If this formula is true, then humankind's religious experience, an experience rooted in a shared primordial reality, can be deciphered and understood. The ambiguity of sacred texts or myths could be, in effect, clarified when read in terms of common humanity. Hermeneutics takes up this proposition presented by phenomenology and answers it with a proposition of its own: a consistent and unified human nature. The question remaining, of course, is how this cohesive and unified human nature is to be defined within a discipline.

The academy of the period immediately following the Second World War experienced a number of challenges to its enduring structure; not the least of which was a larger and (by the standards of the 1940s and 1950s) more diverse student body. Many intellectuals who fled the Nazis, such as Joachim Wach, found themselves in the colleges and universities of the United States. These intellectuals, unlike the majority of their North American colleagues who kept the study of religion bound to a missiology, brought with them a sense of interdisciplinarity which allowed them to invent new disciplines and fields of study. In the case of Joachim Wach, who fled the Nazis in the 1930s, phenomenology, history, psychology, and sociology came together in the study of religion. Wach's sociology of religion offered the social "other" who not only stood outside the West in some remote and exotic part of the world, but also the social "other" who is, in effect, inside the West.

In many respects it was Eliade himself who, having come from Romania to the University of Chicago, extended this insider "other" and the dialogue between empiricism and phenomenology. Eliade's arrival in Chicago to give the Haskell Lectures in 1956 marked the beginnings of a new endeavor, characterized by an anti-methodology for the study of religion which would change the shape of studies in religion, art, literature, and philosophy. One can see how Eliade is a child of both an intellectual history, marked by paradigms of the Western academy, and of a geographical history, Romania. In his book *Significations: Signs, Symbols, and Images in the Interpretation of Religion*, Charles H. Long takes the reader aside in what he calls an "Excursus" to "relate a personal experience." He describes finding a book written by Morris Jastrow Jr, which, in its arrangement of chapters, outlined the author's graduate studies in religion at the University of Chicago under the direction of Joachim Wach. His reading of this book, published in 1902 before the traumas of the twentieth century, pressed Long to wonder if Wach knew of the book and, if he did, why he had not mentioned it. This question leads Long to think about the intellectual and historical context for the study of religion. Earlier in this Excursus, Long discussed Max Muller's intellectual milieu and his connection to the Aryan myth through the exploration of Indo-European languages and myths. Just as the Aryan myth provided the backdrop for Muller's work, the American myth, in its powerful decline, gives historians of religion a socio-political context to address:

> The myth of America as a land of innocent immigrants from Europe who came to a virgin land no longer has the power to state the reality of the human case for us. The rise of other orientations regarding the peopling of this land and the appearance of new structures and sources of power within the ethnic communities of this land, though seen as political realities, are more often than not religious statements about the nature of human reality.[21]

Why does Long oppose these "religious statements" to political realities? To begin answering the question, one needs to understand what Long means by the "religious." The religious is, for Long, like Eliade, the moment in human existence when the questions of identity and affiliation intersect. In other words, who I am is contingent upon where and when I am in relation to the sacred: "In the last analysis, we are attempting to find those existential structures of the life of human communities across space and time which concretely gave and give expression to who and what we are in the scheme of things."[22] The point being made here is consistent with the trajectory of thought in the study of the history of religion in general as it relates to the retreat of the sacred. Subjectivities are constructed "concretely" through the events in a life and the range of interpretive strategies (narratives) available to understand those events – the two never are isomorphic. What Long tells us is that the study of religion, the history of religion, is the space in which the events and the narratives undergo inquiry. For instance, in the Excursus, Long defines the study of the history of religions at Chicago as having four nodal points: Mircea Eliade, a Romanian, whose thought was formed in a country with a Slavic origin and Latin culture; Joseph Kitagawa, a man of Japanese descent, who was held in an internment camp during the Second World War; Jonathan Z. Smith, a Jewish scholar, who was caught between two traditions, the Hellenistic and Hebraic; and Charles H. Long, an African-American, who, in telling this portion of the history at Chicago, draws upon Eliade's deep sense of the "Other." As Long tells the reader, all four were articulated as "others" within the American myth. Yet they somehow came together in that experience of "otherness" to deconstruct the myth, as it appeared, and to extend a line of inquiry into the tension between the existential and the systematic:

But one does not need to become like us, or imitate us, for this discourse to proceed. One needs only to ponder the meaning of the other in the interpretation, description, and understanding of our data. And this could be the "wholly other" in Rudolf Otto's work or the "vague somewhat" that opposes us as "something other" in the words of Gerardus van der Leeuw, or that "other" which constitutes the world of the Orientals and the primitives. In every case, for ideological and methodological reasons, the "other" has become another kind of other. ... New discourse concerning the meaning of religion – a discourse whose possibility is present in America and in its departments of religion – will occur when Americans experience the "otherness" of America; only then will the scholars in religion be able to understand that human intercourse with the world of sacred realities is, hermeneutically speaking, one way, and probably the most profound way, of meeting and greeting our brothers and sisters who form and have formed our species for these several millennia.[23]

These meetings can be understood in terms of Long's lexicon as "contact." Not only do the overarching narratives meet, but the specificities, people with unique and varied existential experiences, meet as well. This "meeting" also has attached to it a "greeting" which was not present when agents of colonialization met indigenous people. The greeting entails recognizing an "otherness" without necessarily understanding or categorizing "otherness." When Long speaks hermeneutically, he is speaking an Eliadean hermeneutics – a hermeneutics which is founded on a non-Hegelian dialectic.

SACRED REALITIES

Eliade's hermeneutics differs from the dialectical hermeneutics of Friedrich Schleiermacher and Wilhelm Dilthey in one important manner of function. Eliade's hermeneutics seeks a synthesis in the archetypal symbols or patterns of human consciousness which will ultimately reveal the sacred within the "concrete," and will not reveal an understanding (*verstehen*) within a linear history marching toward its completion. For Eliade, religion's foundation is mortared with transcultural and transtemporal symbols. These symbols are, in turn, registered or inscribed on the human person via a cohesive human nature formed through the experience of the sacred and culminating in consciousness itself. Armed with an anti-methodology, Eliade manages to introduce alongside an Enlightenment notion of (linear) history a non-temporal or anti-temporal hermeneutic which is structured in liturgical time. Symbols, then, have eternality which consistently point to the sacred. To return for a moment to Long's "greeting," one can see the relationship between Eliade's eternality of symbols and Long's "world of sacred realities." It is true, for both Eliade and Long, that all human beings experience the sacred – how they experience the sacred, however, is not uniform. Since it is the case that human beings experience the sacred in multiform ways and not that the sacred is experienced in any one consistent way, the historian of religion needs to always maintain that rift in "bringing together," to use Eliade's language, the sacred and the profane. In paying attention to the rift, one "greets" and not enslaves, one "greets" and not murders, one "greets" and not converts.

Eliade's works oscillate between epiphanies and methodologies. His personal experiences of the sacred as a child in Romania have a line of filiation with his scholarship, exfoliating the presence of the sacred in the profane across the world's religions. In his processes of exfoliation, Eliade turns his inquiry to the human person, to the subject as he or she stands in relation to the sacred, the ultimate. These epiphanies and methodologies seem, at times, to come together in the morphology which Eliade inherited from Wolfgang von Goethe. The structure and ultimacy of the sacred is analogous to plant morphology. One finds an *urpflanze*, a primordial plant or symbol, which decodes the ordering of experience. In this sense, Eliade's epiphanies and methodologies are merely philosophical approximations in so far as neither approach yields a final reconciliation of the sacred and the profane.

> The intimate relationship of various external parts of plants – such as leaves, calyx, corolla, and stamens – which develop one after another, and apparently from one another, has long been recognized by naturalists in a general way. Indeed, it has even been studied in detail, and the process by which one and the same organ makes its appearance in multifarious forms has been named the *metamorphosis of plants*.[24]

> Because it is a hierophany, it reveals some modality of the sacred; because it is historical, it reveals some attitude man has toward the sacred. … Every hierophany we look at is also an historical fact. Every manifestation of the sacred takes place in some historical situation. Even the most personal and transcendent mystical experiences are affected by the age in which they occur.[25]

Contrary to the thinking of many Eliadean scholars, this *urpflanze* reveals a *quantity* (an

historical condition) of being human rather than a *quality* or *characteristic* of being human. In other words, the "Other" is in history and will always remain "Other." Although all human beings experience an ultimate, a "vague somewhat," which crafts existence, that "vague somewhat" is not, because of the interdict of history, universally shared; nor is the experience of that vague somewhat universally shared. Eliade's hermeneutic and, by implication, his morphology defer a moment of closure which is endemic to Western scholarship. In this sense, Eliade's epiphanies and methodologies are, to some extent, misnomers in that neither of the two result in a synthesis of understanding. Consequently, Eliade's work is (mis)read as supplying an holistic view of religion, or else he is dismissed as being a mystic or dilettante.

Eliade was well aware of the potential criticisms his methodology would attract, and he went to some length to explain the difficulties of method in *Patterns in Comparative Religion*: "The religious historian must trace not only the history of a given hierophany, but must first of all understand and explain the modality of the sacred that the hierophany discloses."[26] Here Eliade raises two difficulties: the first is the ever-present element of chance in recovering the "scraps of evidence," or the religious data; and the second, the question "are we right to speak of different modalities of the sacred?"[27] The answer to the first problem is somewhat self-evident: religious historians must rely on finding or happening upon the objects or texts of a community's religious practices. The second problem is philosophically difficult. Eliade juxtaposes the experience of the sacred as it is understood and explained by the initiates *with* that same experience of the sacred as it is experienced by the masses. In what may seem a rather undemocratic tendency, Eliade, though seeing both as valuable experiences of the sacred, favors the experience of the initiate over that of the masses. He does, however, conclude that the two experiences come together in a fuller expression of the hierophany, and that it is this coming together or fitting together of the hierophanies which results in a pattern of the sacred:

> That those modalities exist is proved by the fact that a given hierophany may be lived and interpreted quite differently by the religious elite and by the rest of the community. For the throng who come to the temple of Kalighat in Calcutta every autumn Durga is simply a goddess of terror to whom goats are sacrificed; but for a few initiated saktas Durga is the manifestation of cosmic life in constant and violent regeneration … which is the true meaning of Durga and Siva – what is deciphered by the initiates, or what is taken up by the mass of the faithful?[28]

What is important for Eliade is the multivalent nature of the sacred as it becomes manifest within the "same" historical moment. Not only does the sacred emerge differently within a given religion, or a given ritual for that matter, but the emergence of the sacred is never complete within the profane. In this sense, the notion that the sacred is the dialectical inversion (an Hegelian dialectic) of the profane is misleading since the movement of the sacred into the profane is never the "same" or complete, because while the sacred is eternal and uncontainable the profane is mutable. This leads Eliade to say that the "safest method, clearly, is to make use of all these kinds of evidence (symbols, myths, rites, or divine forms), omitting no important type and asking ourselves what *meaning* is revealed by each of these hierophanies."[29] In *The Quest: History and Meaning in Religion*, Eliade refers to this as the bipartition of the world which religious experience must presuppose. The bipartition of the world into the sacred and the profane is not an altogether clear dualism, with one implying the other. There are, Eliade tells us, two types of sacrality:

68

> Suffice to say that it is not a question of an embryonic dualism, for the profane is transmuted into the sacred by the dialectic of hierophany. On the other hand, numerous processes of desacralization retransform the sacred into the profane. But we find the exemplary opposition of the sacred and the profane in the numberless list of binary antagonisms, together with the oppositions male–female, heaven–earth, etc. To look at it more closely, it is evident that when sexual antagonism between two types of sacrality is expressed in a religious context, it is less a question of the opposition sacred–profane than it is of the antagonism between two types of sacralities, one exclusive to men and the other proper to women.[30]

Eliade continues this point by referring to the rituals of the indigenous men and women of Australia. In the rituals surrounding transitions from puberty to adulthood, Aboriginal males are separated from the world of their mothers and of women in an effort to make them part of the "sacred" world of men, which is kept secret from the women. At the same time, the women have their own rituals of separation, which they similarly keep secret from the men. Eliade's point here is that the sacred remains constant, while the manifestations of that sacred change. In this sense the two types of sacrality one finds in opposition are a masculine sacrality and a feminine sacrality. What is implied here (Eliade does not pursue the point) is that the sacred "transcends," as it were, profane categories and that the feminine sacrality is no less sacred than the masculine sacrality.

It is these implications, or folds, in Eliade's writing which open his work to a postmodern reading, in the sense that the minor narratives, such as the feminine sacrality, carry with them a degree of sacrality "equal" to that of a major narrative, specifically the masculine sacrality. Furthermore, the minor narratives which permeate the history of religion pressure the discursive structure to relinquish its hold on the sacred. "We must," Eliade writes in *Patterns in Comparative Religion*, "get used to the idea of recognizing hierophanies absolutely everywhere, in every area of psychology, economic, spiritual and sacred life."[31] Not only do we have to get accustomed to seeing hierophanies everywhere, as Eliade suggests, we must, at the same time, become accustomed to affording the (non)concept of sacrality to things which seem quite ordinary or, perhaps, profane or obscene. The sacred power, the ultimate, as it is transfigures the profane, can reside, as Eliade tells us, anywhere. These manifestations of the sacred are not always of the mythico-symbolic order; in fact, the minor narratives derive from local hierophanies – hierophanies which do not automatically illustrate a connection with other hierophanies in terms of organic coexistence, symbolic analogy, or functional symmetry. Instead these local hierophanies exist in the hollows and folds of the major narrative and, often through their subjugation, verify a hierarchy of ideas. Hierophanies everywhere and sacrality everywhere as well leave the notion of the sacred–profane dualism incomplete. Whereas the hierophany was assumed to be a manifestation of the sacred, perhaps even a description or testament of the presence of the sacred, sacrality "everywhere" suggests that hierophanies merely mark the absence of the sacred and not its moment of plenitude:

> Finally, it is important to note that the mediation between the contraries also presents a great variety of solutions. There is opposition, clash, and combat, but in certain cases the conflict is resolved in a union which produces a "third term," while in the others the polarities seem to coexist paradoxically in a *coincidentia oppositorum*, or they are transcended, i.e., radically

> abolished or rendered unreal, incomprehensible, or meaningless. This variety of solutions to the problems raised by the mediation between the contraries – and we must add also the radically "dualistic" positions, which refuse any mediation – merits special investigation. For if it is true that any solution found to the crisis provoked by the awareness of polarities implies somehow the beginning of wisdom, the very multiplicity and the extreme variety of such solutions arouse the critical reflection and prepare for the coming of philosophy.[32]

This coming of philosophy is preceded by the advent of the "Other." Eliade's anti-methodology is not challenged by the rigors of philosophy; rather, his anti-methodology is challenged by how well it manages to recognize the sacred of the Other:

> But if the peoples of the West are no longer the only ones to "make" history, their spiritual and cultural values will no longer enjoy the privileged place, to say nothing of the unquestioned authority, that they enjoyed some generations ago. These values are now being analyzed, compared, and judged by non-Westerners. On their side, Westerners are being increasingly led to study, reflect on, and understand the spiritualities of Asia and the archaic world. These discoveries and contacts must be extended through dialogues. But to be genuine and fruitful, a dialogue cannot be limited to empirical and utilitarian language. A true dialogue must deal with the central values in the cultures of the participants.[33]

Mircea Eliade's "new humanism" calls upon scholars in the humanities to widen their understandings of the "existential situation of 'being in the world'" – an existential situation which is for us marked by the death of the God of Christendom. It is an understanding brought on by the forceful abandoning of the reductive positivistic methodologies which, for Eliade, have resulted in the uninspired "collecting, publishing, and analyzing of religious data."[34] For Eliade, these familiar activities, grounded in empiricism, are to be left aside in favor of a new work, a hermeneutic, which will make "the meaning of religious documents intelligible to the mind of modern man."[35] This call to think hermeneutically, issued in Eliade's essay "History of Religion and a New Humanism," taken to its extreme limits within academic circles, is intended not only for those scholars who exclusively study the history of religions, but for "scholars" in the humanities in general.

What concerns Eliade in this essay is the loss of the cultural specificity of religious phenomena and the subsequent loss of *meaning* when Western categories are superimposed on non-Western religious "phenomena." Whereas, the "old" humanism sought to unite all people together under the yoke of the *sui generis* nature of being human, Eliade's "new" humanism, it can be argued, is an insertion of the proposition that the *sui generis* nature of being human is not only empirically unproveable through the collection of ethnographic research, artwork, sociological inquiry and other means of data compilation, it is, more importantly, oppressive to those whose central values are unintelligible within Western schematizations: "the peoples of Asia have recently re-entered history; ... the so-called primitive peoples are preparing to make their appearance on the horizon of greater history (that is, they are seeking to become *active subjects* of history instead of *passive objects*, as they have been hitherto)."[36]

This, then, leads to an intellectual and political dispute in the sense that Eliade's work over the years has come to mean the opposite of this. That is to say, Eliade's "new humanism" has been understood by many in the field of religious studies and art criticism as the "old

humanism" resurrected or, at least, refurbished, barring a direct commonalty – an essential human nature which gives rise to moral and social orders which have a degree of consistency across time and culture – in favor of an indirect commonalty – the creative imagination. While Eliade's immense concern with the power of Western categories to overwhelm and silence those non-Western people is to some extent addressed in this conventional reading of Eliade's "new humanism," there still persists this problem of representing the *other*. On the one hand, as scholars responding to Eliade's call for a "new humanism" have been consciences as to the power dynamic between Western and non-Western people, it is still worth asking if that attentiveness to the power dynamic is adequate in addressing the representation of the *other* in the study of religion and in the study of art; in addition to that particular point one may ask whether Eliade was calling for a move toward the "universal" creative imagination, as some have suggested, or was this "new humanism" something quite different from that totalizing concept? In order to begin an inquiry into this dispute, it is necessary to locate what Eliade calls "discoveries and contacts" which will make clearer the stakes, both intellectual and political, of weaving together phenomena and understanding.

While Malraux re-imagines the dialectical relationship between art and religion, it is Eliade, in a later essay concerning a new humanism, who presents art as a religious phenomenon, existing on a separate *plane of reference*. Of all Eliade's cryptic statements about the nature of art and religion, this one in particular raises the question of how Eliade thought art and religion are connected. Eliade continues to give further definition to art's separate *plane of reference*. It is not, Eliade tells us, a "physical universe of immediate experience" implying "their nonreality"; it is, rather, another universe altogether, one which Eliade feels has been sufficiently discussed to warrant proceeding to his next point about the autonomy of the work of art. But has this *mode of being* undergone sufficient scrutiny in Eliade's work? Although Eliade states that the problem of art's being has been "sufficiently" discussed, there remains in Eliade's formulations a degree of insufficiency in art and an uncertainty concerning art's *mode of being*. Eliade struggles against what he perceives to be an attempt on the part of scholars to eradicate the specificity of the "Other," religious experience, and art by setting in motion formal categories or overarching narratives which render the "Other," religious experience, and art-object exhausted: "We must never lose sight of one of the fundamental principles of modern science: *the scale creates the phenomenon*."[37]

As one reads through this essay, what becomes apparent is a tension between autonomy and contingency. Eliade's work, in general, is significantly affected by this tension in so far as the sacred and the profane are simultaneously always and never "connected." The same simultaneity presents itself whenever Eliade is pressed to articulate a rupture in the plane of reference. His quarrel with those who attempt to "explicate" literary works, for instance, is part of his ongoing resistance to reductive methodologies which reduce works to "one or another origin – infantile trauma, glandular accident, or economic, social, or political situations."[38] With an acknowledgment of Eliade's flippancy, one can easily see Eliade's sympathy with "hermeneutics" and his antipathy for any method which claims to completely render the "other," religious experience, and works of art in its entirety. Of course, "hermeneutics," too, can easily be called upon to defend itself against the charge of reductionism. Here one finds Eliade enmeshed in a difficult situation – caught between two equally passionate needs, one for understanding and the Other for mystery:

71

> We have no intention of developing a methodology of the science of religions here. The problem is far too complex to be treated in a few pages. But we think it useful to repeat that the *homo religiosus* represents the "total man"; hence, the science of religions must become a total discipline in the sense that it must use, integrate, and articulate the results obtained by the various methods of approaching a religious phenomenon. It is not enough to grasp the meaning of a religious phenomenon in a certain culture and, consequently, to decipher its "message" (for every religious phenomenon constitutes a "cipher"); it is also necessary to study and understand its "history," that is, to unravel its changes and modifications and, ultimately, to elucidate its contribution to the entire culture.[39]

Eliade finishes his point with a look toward the future in which two competing modes of inquiry will be eventually reconciled to the extent that the tension produced will, in some way, foster processes of discovery and contact:

> it would be naive to suppose that the tension between those who try to understand the *essence* and the *structures* and those whose only concern is the *history* of religious phenomena will one day be completely done away with. But such tension is creative. It is by virtue of it that the science of religions will escape dogmatism and stagnation.[40]

Has Eliade set aside the question of representing the "Other"? Clearly, Eliade is not satisfied with the available array of methodologies which enclose the "Other" and reduce the "Other" to a consequence of Western categories. Eliade's belief in a hermeneutical enterprise avoids the all-too-easy ethnographic response to the "Other" and situates this "Other" in history. The "Other" in history, as it were, is an (un)communicable "Other" in so far as the idiosyncratic nature of that "Other's" materiality refuses erasure. The quest for a new humanism can easily be characterized as a new communication minus the certainty of the Western subject. As we have already seen, Eliade's new humanism exists within at least two competing gravitational fields: simulation and dissimulation. This new humanism is precariously poised between revealing the essence of a religious phenomenon and being fooled by its disguise in history. This opposition is not altogether uncommon in Eliade's thought; in fact, one can argue, it is the foundation of his thought, the *coincidentia oppositorum*.

PARASACRALIZATION

Malraux's study of painting and Eliade's study of patterns in comparative religion often mark the point of departure of the sacred, as a transcendent reality, from the profane, as the concrete. I have offered a rather different reading which takes up this departure, not as a moment of desacralization, but a moment of parasacralization. Malraux and Eliade both labor under the notion of the bi-partition of the world. One could argue that Eliade was invested not so much in a transcendent sacred as in an historical sacred. One could not make that argument on behalf of Malraux. In the end, the argument does not work for Eliade either. Eliade was tied to the bi-furcation of the world and, in that sense, Thomas J.J. Altizer is correct – Eliade is a negative theologian, but not for the reason Altizer gives. First, as Eliade and Malraux describe it, there was never a division of the world into two parts. Second, there

72

was no division of the world and *then* a coming together of the world, as Altizer describes. In effect, the dialectic here forces one to argue that it has not happened yet (Malraux), or that it is happening (Eliade), or that it has happened (Altizer). Instead, we are around the sacred in the sense that human existence drifts across a multitude of ultimacies. The sacred or, as it undergoes disfigurement, the parasacred, is the condition of human existence and not the content of it.

CHAPTER 5

Para Shoah

All memory has the taste of poison.

(Edmond Jabès, The Book of Questions)

Driven by thirst, I eyed a fine icicle outside the window, within hand's reach. I opened the window and broke off the icicle but at once a large heavy guard prowling outside brutally snatched it away from me. "Warum?" I asked him in my poor German. "Hier ist kein warum," he replied, pushing me inside with a shove.

(Primo Levi, "On the Bottom," Survival in Auschwitz)

You are informed that human beings endowed with language [*doués de langage*] were placed in a situation such that none of them is now able to tell about it. Most of them disappeared then, and the survivors rarely speak about it. When they do speak about it, their testimony bears upon a minute part of this situation [*Quand ils en parlent, leur témoignage ne porte que sur une infime partie de cette situation*]. How can you know that the situation itself existed? That it is not the fruit of your informant's imagination? Either the situation did not exist as such. Or else it did exist, in which case your informant's testimony is false, either because he or she should have disappeared, or else because he or she should remain silent, or else because, if he or she does speak, he or she can bear witness only to the particular experience he had, it remaining to be established whether this was a component of the situation in question.

"I have analyzed thousands of documents. I have tirelessly pursued specialists and historians with

my questions. I have tried in vain to find a single former deportee capable of proving to me that he had really seen, with his own eyes, a gas chamber" (Faurisson in Pierre-Naquet, 1981: 81). To have "really seen with his own eyes" a gas chamber would be the condition which gives one the authority to say that it exists and to persuade the unbeliever. Yet it is still necessary to prove that the gas chamber was used to kill at the time it was seen. The only acceptable proof that is was used to kill is that one died from it. But if one is dead, one cannot testify that it is on account of the gas chamber – The plaintiff complains that he has been fooled about the existence of gas chambers, fooled that is, about the so-called Final Solution. His argument is: in order for a place to be identified as a gas chamber, the only eyewitness I will accept would be a victim of this gas chamber; now, according to my opponent, there is no victim that is not dead; otherwise, this gas chamber would not be what he or she claims it to be. There is, therefore, no gas chamber [*il n'y a donc pas de chambre à gaz*].

(Jean-François Lyotard, The Differend)

WITNESSES AND EVENTS

Faurisson's disturbing challenge to the facticity of the Shoah begins with a calling forth of a witness to testify to the effects of Zyklon B. It is, we have learned all too well, impossible to bring forward such a witness to testify on *behalf* of those who died in the gas-chamber who is himself or herself not dead. It is through this hyperbolic juridical circumstance that Faurisson attempts to arrive at what he considers to be the unquestionable historical truth – the non-existence of the gas-chambers. By invoking the sacrality of memory, in the form of a witness,

Faurisson reveals that the Shoah is an impossible narratological situation.[1] If just one witness to the gas-chamber were to step forward from history and recall the chamber's interior, its death, then sufficient proof would be in that moment of recollection.

Faurisson's denial of the gas-chamber is, oddly, both an affirmation and a renunciation of memory's depth and rootedness in the sacred, in the sense that memory is thought to be complete, epistemologically sound, incorrigible, validated by the continuity of the sacred, and the measure of truth. It can be argued at the same time, however, that memory merely can attest to the abyss, the lapses in narrative, the pervasive forgetfulness of history. It is this duality that brings to the surface a significant contrast between remembering and not forgetting.

Memory, after the Shoah, has lost its place within the realm of the sacred. One of the many troubling questions which arises after the Shoah concerns the understanding of memory's long-held juridical connection to truth and to the sacred. This is perhaps why the initial Holocaust memorials were not permanent or fixed to a landscape, as they are today. Instead, they were narratives, the *Yizkor Bikher*. James E. Young likens these "books" to "symbolic tombstones" for those who died and did not leave "corpses to inter."[2] Young continues his analysis of the *Yizkor Bikher* by way of the interior site of the memorial over and against the memorial as an exterior site. Before the memorials occupied a landscape, they were sanctioned by and occupied an interior landscape of the mind, and it is here that one can asked: What is memory? What is forgetting? What is recollection? What does it mean to remember and forget?

Answers to these questions concerning juridical memory, some would argue, begin with

the Greeks and their mythology. After all, was it not Tiresias who did *not* forget his own murder?

Œdipus: What tales? I must hear them all?
Chorus: How he met his death through traveling vagabonds.
Œdipus: I've heard that too. We have no witnesses, however.[3]

The preservation of memory finds its form in and as history through Herodotus. History, in the Greek sense, was not forgetting (not dying) what had taken place. In Plato's *Republic* the Myth of Er speaks to this deep connection between death and forgetfulness. It is Er who experiences death without suffering the casualty of memory:

> After all the souls had chosen their lives, they went forward to Lachesis in the same order in which they had made their choices, and she assigned to each the daimon it had chosen as guardian of its life and fulfiller of its choice. This daimon first led the soul under the hand of Clotho as it turned the revolving spindle to confirm the fate that the lottery and its own choice had given it. After receiving her touch, he led the soul to the spinning Atropos, to make what had been spun irreversible. Then, without turning around, they went from under the Throne of Necessity and, when all of them had passed through, they traveled to the Plain of Forgetfulness in burning and choking, terrible heat, for it was empty of trees and earthly vegetation. And there, beside the River of Unheeding, whose water no vessel can hold, they camped, for night was coming on. All of them had to drink a certain measure of this water, but those who weren't saved by reason drank more than that, and as each of them drank, he forgot

everything and went to sleep. But around midnight there was a clap of thunder and an earthquake, and they were suddenly carried away from there, this way and that, up to their births, like shooting stars. Er himself was forbidden to drink from the water. All the same, he didn't know how he had come back to his body, except that waking suddenly he saw himself lying on the pyre at dawn.

And so, Glaucon, his story wasn't lost but preserved, and it would save us, if we were persuaded by it, for we would then make a good crossing of the River of Unheeding, and our souls wouldn't be defiled. But if we are persuaded by me, we'll believe that the soul is immortal and able to endure every evil and every good, and we'll always hold to the upward path, practicing justice with reason every way.[4]

Although one may find juridical memory to be uniquely Greek, it is the Jews who forge an idea of memory as history through a conversion of memory into remembrance, *Zakhor*.[5] In other words, Jewish history is not predicated on the *not forgetting*, but on the inclusion of God in the events of the world. History, then, is God remembered: theophany. It is this tension between the Greek accessible memory and the Jewish inaccessible memory which will shape our discussion of the sacred and memory.

Mircea Eliade's *Myth and Reality* provides us with a beginning through this tension and labyrinth of memory by taking up the history of memory in terms of Greek mythology. For Eliade, memory (*mnemne*) and forgetfulness (*amnesia*) are aspects of mythology in so far as one is the dialectical inversion of the other within the deep structures of human experience. Here, there are two primary sites, one of primordial memory and the other of individual

memory. In this understanding, memory is separated from the profane. The truth, knowledge, for the Greeks, was a process of remembering that which the soul already knew:

For only the soul that has beheld truth may enter into our human form, passing from a plurality of perceptions to a unity gathered together by reasoning – and such understanding is the recollection of those things which our souls beheld aforetime as they journeyed with their god, looking down upon the things which now we suppose to be, and gazing up to that which truly is.[6]

Recollection (*anamnesis*), however, is that which interrupts the smoothness of the dialectic and the depth of the structure, in that the soul does not recollect the totality of memory: "Memory, Plotinus held, is for those who have forgotten. For those who have forgotten, remembering is a virtue; but the perfect never lose the vision of truth and they have no need to remember."[7] It is here that one finds the difference between recollection (*anamnesis*) and memory (*mnemne*). Memory is complete and of the soul, while recollection is partial and fragmentary. Faurisson's point, if I understand him correctly, is that those who actually died in the gas-chamber are the only ones who can speak as to the truth of its existence. Faurisson links memory with existence in a peculiar way when he makes an event's facticity contingent upon the process of recollection. This brings us to the relationship between knowledge and memory. Of course, for the ancient Greeks, knowledge was memory. That is to say, what one knows is an effect of the soul's memory. This is particularly true of the relationship between knowledge and memory developed in the *Meno* and *Phaedrus of Plato*.

Certainty is the region of death, uncertainty the valley of life.

(Edmond Jabès, *The Book of Questions*)

Faurrison's memory has a depth which is not altogether apparent if one does not see knowledge as a consequence of memory. The surface of memory, however, suggests lack of depth, the absence of an original reality. In this sense, memory does not have the connotations of another world or an original reality which is somehow brought forth through remembering. One who remembers completely is a traveler between these two worlds, between life and death. Such a vision of the one who remembers, one who bears witness to an event, eclipses the surface of memory: "The fountain Lethe, forgetfulness, is a necessary part of the realm of death. The dead are those who have lost their memories."[8] Those who cannot bear witness to the gas-chamber, to return to Faurisson, have lost their memories to death. Like the waters from the fountain Lethe, Zyklon B erased memories. Therefore, there is no memory of the gas-chamber; there, in its place, is death. Faurisson's call to "witness" is a call to bear witness to death, to call forth memories which have been eradicated by and in death. In this regard, Faurisson is calling out for Tiresias, Amphiaraus, or Aethalides, each of whom has unchangeable memories in an eternal existence.

Since we do not have a Tiresias, an Amphiaraus, or an Aethalides to bear witness to the event(s) of the Nazi gas-chamber or to death itself, we can be concerned only about the gas-

chamber. That is to say, we can(not) talk only *about* the gas-chamber, not of it. It is here that parasacrality conjoins with ethics to form a paraethics, an ethics about ethics or ethics beside and around itself. Ethics suffers from the same dialectical thinking which affects politics. Events are suspended between two oppositional points which are drawn together through a defined process of reconciliation of polarities. These two oppositional points are, actually, thought of as two interdependent realms: the real and the actual. Ethics is then traditionally presented as a way of tying together the two realms (opposing ends of the same string), or resolving the tension or distance between the two. What would happen, conceptually, were the string cut into an infinity of segments? What is/was the continuity keeping the string single, one uninterrupted line holding the two points in opposition? History? Sacrality? God? Eternity? All of these could produce continuity, depending on the narrative deployed with the bi-partition of the world. It is the nature of narrative to tie points together. In this sense, anything could initiate a narrative that would explain any event. The move, however, is not to find the grandest of narratives, but to recognize at least two important points: anything (history, deity, class, race, gender, sexuality, etc.) can produce a grand narrative which can account, with equal proficiency, for the continuity of all events; *nothing* can account for discontinuity, given that *accounting for* is an invocation of continuity – the continuity of discontinuity, if you will. Gilles Deleuze and Felix Guattari begin their book *What Is Philosophy?* with the discontinuity of the concept:

There are no simple concepts. Every concept has components and is defined by them. It there-fore has a combination [*chiffre*]. It is a multiplicity, although not every multiplicity is conceptual. There is no concept with only one component. Even the first concept, the one with which a philosophy "begins," has several components, because it is not obvious that philosophy must have a beginning, and if it does determine one, it must combine it with a point of view or a ground [*une raison*]. Not only do Descartes, Hegel, and Feuerbach not begin with the same concept, they do not have the same concept of beginning. Every concept is at least double or triple, etc. Neither is there a concept possessing every component, since this would be chaos pure and simple. Even so-called universals as concepts must escape the chaos by circumscribing a universe that explains them (contemplation, reflection, communication). Every concept has an irregular contour defined by the sum of its components, which is why, from Plato to Bergson, we find the idea of the concept being a matter of articulation, of cutting and cross-cutting. The concept is a whole because it totalizes its components, but it is a fragmentary whole. Only on this condition can it escape the mental chaos constantly threatening it, stalking it, trying to reabsorb it.[9]

The prefix *para* indicates this complexity, this beyond, this extra, this alteration of the continuous line found in things such as subjectivity, ethics, politics, experience. It is not so much a continuity as it is an erring or a wandering around the not: "The question of the not, therefore, is a question of the unthinkable that we can neither think nor not think. In thinking not, thought approaches a limit that inhabits it *as if* from within. This exteriority, which is interior, rends thought, leaving it forever incomplete."[10] It is this beyond, extra, disruption, or alteration, which Jean-François Lyotard identifies in "Discussion, or Phrasing 'After Auschwitz'" as speculative dialectics (dialectical logic), that I will attend to first through Gilles Deleuze's (non)concept of "singularity–event." Just as Gilles Deleuze comes to question the univocity (totalization) of actualization (the concretization of knowledge within

79

language games), Lyotard, too, working out of Adorno's *Negative Dialectics*, comes to question the shaping rules which govern the linking of phrases within discursive structures or language-compounds. It is the linkages surrounding the death-camp which set in motion Lyotard's "Phrasing 'After Auschwitz'." Another issue presents itself and, subsequently, will be taken up as the beyond, extra, or alteration of speculative dialectics as it relates to politics, or the polis that *wills* its own end. The culmination of this task will be an argument against a unilateral politics (the polis's willing of its own end) and an argument for a para or pagan (*pagus*) politics which will, unlike the prior construction that is based upon a monological or one-sided infrastructure (pure ethics), have a heterological, or multiple and varied, infrastructure (paraethics) out of which occurs a respect for *differends* and for the multiplicity of justice.

   One drifts, then, from the synthesizing effects of the monological infrastructure (Lyotard's "Grand Narrative," or speculative dialectics) and toward the Deleuzean supple segmentarity of lines or quantum flows which offer the possibility of another sense of time, another subjectivity, and another politics.[11] There is, I will argue, a correspondence between Deleuze's and Lyotard's understanding of the epistemological question in so far as both philosophers take up and juxtapose the two "Kants." Kant, as Lyotard indicates, is both an epilogue to modernity and a prologue to postmodernity. Kant, sitting astride these two conceptual *regimens*, poses an interesting and equally troubling question of ethics and politics which focuses on the incommensurability of the idea of reason and the concept. Both Deleuze and Lyotard recognize the Kantian problem as a problem concerning linkages within and between categories (faculties) or *genres* . Central to the Kantian problem is the issue of first principles or grounding – the ground(ing) of the subject and the ground(ing) of the political. Each of these ground(ing)s, if you will, is a nodal point along a segmented line(s). The first point is the "autonomous" subject who "knows" the ethical, a priori; and the second point is the polis which is the alleged culmination of humanity; the self-presence of the polis (we allow) allows itself to *will* its own telos. A Deleuzean and, related, Lyotardian rewriting of this Kantian problematic entails an encounter with this culminating moment identified as Hegelian dialectics – or, that which synthesizes the phrases of Kant's *Begebenheit*, or event, into a fixed historical reality. Lyotard writes in his essay "The Sign of History":

> The Begebenheit, which is a *datum in* experience at least, if not *of* experience, must be the index of the idea of Free causality. With this *Begebenheit* we must get as close as possible to the abyss to be crossed between mechanism on the one hand and liberty or finality on the other, between the domain of the sensory world and the field of the suprasensible – and we should be able to leap across it without suppressing it, by fixing the status of the historico-political – a status which may be inconsistent and indeterminate, but which can be spoken, and which is even irrefutable.[12]

What is this leap if it is not the dialectic, or the signifier in search of a signified?

Lyotard's "Discussions, or Phrasing 'After Auschwitz'" concerns itself with the same questioning of the dialectic or leap that concerns Adorno in his text *Negative Dialectics*, in which he writes: "In the camps death has a novel horror; since Auschwitz, fearing death means fearing worse than death"[13] This chapter will discuss the epistemological gap between the idea of reason and the concept and the speculative discourses which have, in modernity, synthesized the two; the chapter will first explore Deleuze's logic of sense or, more

specifically, the (non)concepts of singularity and event, and then Lyotard's *différend* in order to arrive at a discussion of phrases about the anonym Auschwitz. Another subjectivity, another politics, another ethics, are perpetually bothered and hampered by the extant and rigid politics, ethics, subjectivity or Kant's nodal points and modernity's tendency to synthesize discourses through the Hegelian dialectic.

In prefacing his collection of musings entitled *Dialogues*, Gilles Deleuze writes against a Kantian ground-zero and a Hegelian totality: "Every multiplicity grows from the middle, like a blade of grass or the rhizome. We constantly oppose the rhizome to the tree, like two conceptions and even two very different ways of thinking. A line does not go from one point to another, but passes between the points, ceaselessly bifurcating and diverging, like one of Pollock's lines."[14] Achieving another politics, another ethics, another subjectivity, Deleuze argues, necessitates thinking "rhizomically." Contrary to the historical reality constructed by and out of the unifying tendency and binary logic of modernity or Enlightenment thinking, a rhizomic reality lacks a ground-zero or a moment of metaphysical certitude and determinacy by which all phrases (shoots) are linked. Deleuze advances this rhizomic thinking through the (non)concept of singularity – the multiplicity or heterogeneity of the universe of phrases. For Deleuze, the universe of phrases is like a universe of lines; lines which share neither a point of departure nor a point of arrival. Deleuze, in *Dialogues* and *The Logic of Sense*, and, with Guattari, in *A Thousand Plateaus*, is preoccupied with the notion of lines and cracks. In *Dialogues* and, with Guattari, *A Thousand Plateaus*, Deleuze discusses F. Scott Fitzgerald's short story "Crack-up" in which the author describes his life as a collection of fractures represented by a multitude of lines. Fitzgerald, who in this story is looking back on a life of alcoholism and collapse, writes:

Of course all life is a process of breaking down, but the blows that do the dramatic side of the work – the big sudden blows that come or seem to come, from outside – the ones you remember and blame things on and, in moments of weakness, tell your friends about, don't show their effect all at once. There is another sort of blow that comes from within – that you don't feel until it's too late to do anything about it, until you realize with finality that in some regard you will never be as good a man again. The first sort of breakage seems to happen quick – the second kind happens almost without your knowing it but is realized suddenly indeed.[15]

It is, I think, this process of breaking down captured by Fitzgerald which most interests Deleuze. Later in "Crack-up" Fitzgerald uses the image of a cracked plate, with all its divergent lines, to depict the process of living. It is a plate that must be hidden from company and, on the rare occasion that it is used, it rests underneath another plate holding leftovers in the refrigerator. In *A Thousand Plateaus*, Deleuze continues his preoccupation with lines and cracks when he refers to Fitzgerald's alcoholism and turbulent relationship with Zelda[16] as lines of flight:

Beautiful texts. All of the lines are there: the lines of family and friends, of all those who speak, explain, and psychoanalyze, assigning rights and wrongs, of the whole binary machine of the Couple, united or divided, in rigid segmentarity (50 percent). Then there is the line of supple segmentation, from which the alcoholic and the madwoman extract, as from a kiss on the lips and eyes, the multiplication of a double at the limit of what they can endure in their state and with tacit understandings serving them as internal messages. Finally, there is a line of flight, all

the more shared now that they are separated, or vice versa, each of them the clandestine of the other, a double all the more successful now that nothing has importance any longer, now that everything can begin anew, since they have been destroyed but not by each other. Nothing will enter memory, everything was on the lines, in the AND that made one *and* the other imperceptible, without disjunction or conjunction but only a line of flight forever in the process of being drawn, toward a new acceptance, the opposite of renunciation or resignation – a new happiness?[17]

The line of flight (dis)connects the singularity of the universe of phrases to the relationship (event). This anti-Hegelian move is not accomplished by revealing the actual essence of Fitzgerald and Zelda's relationship, but by drawing or extending the line(s) out of and around the relationship as it relates to family and friends – the line of flight, consequently, is a multiple line(s). For Deleuze, the line of flight forever in the process of being drawn is the *para* of (para)ethics and (para)politics because it prohibits the collapse of the universe of phrases into a solid, undifferentiated, discursive mass. If one takes the relationship between Fitzgerald and Zelda to be an *event*, then Deleuze's fascination with it and the short story "Crack-up" becomes a telling moment in his assault on the synthesizing process of the dialectic. The ongoing extension of the line(s) of flight speaks to what Wittgenstein would call the *state of affairs* in so far as the line(s) of flight do not concede to a totality or a determinate language-game. Deleuze and Guattari find an added dimension to the relationship which complicates an all-too-glib explication of it in the discourses of psychology or marriage counseling, for example.

The "Fifteenth Series of Singularities" in *The Logic of Sense* addresses this issue of totalizing discourses or a determinate language-game by setting up a distinction and relation between singularity and event. First, the singularities, Deleuze tells us, are the true transcendental events" [*sont les vrais événements transcendantaux*][18] in that they escape a synthesizing moment or, in other words, never have their potential completely actualized within a discursive structure (Marxism, psychoanalysis). Singularities, as line(s) of flight, do not have a congealed ontos nor do they have a congealed telos. They have, as Lyotard would phrase it, two zero points in much the same way a rhizomic understanding of language posits subterranean unrooted shoots as a metaphor for disunity and multiplicity of logic. Deleuze, early in the chapter, uses the example of a battle that "*hovers over* its own field, being neutral in relation to all its temporal actualizations, neutral and impassive in relation to the victor and the vanquished, the coward and the brave."[19] The battle, seen as hovering above its own field, prohibits a complete or exhaustive actualization through a grounding or an anchoring of *intelligibility* within a cognitive genre (pure referentiality). Deleuze understands this suspension to be an "indifference" to the total(izable) actualization; it is, instead, an event which has an infinite number of singularities bringing it into partial and incomplete positioning within the universe of phrases:

> In the first place, singular–events correspond to heterogeneous series which are organized into a system which is neither stable nor unstable, rather "metastable," endowed with a potential energy wherein the differences between series are distributed. (Potential energy is the energy of the pure event [*l'événement pur*], whereas forms of actualization correspond to the realization of the event) [*tandis que les formes d'actualisation correspondent aux effectuations de*

> *l'événement*]. In the second place, singularities posses a process of auto-unification, always mobile and displaced to the extent that a paradoxical element traverses the series and makes them resonate [*fait résonner*], enveloping the corresponding singular points in a single aleatory point and all emissions, all dice throws, in a single cast [*tous les coups, dans un même lancer*].[20]

If one understands the throw of the dice to be an event, then the combinations on the faces of the dice correspond to the singularities. Before the dice comes to rest any combination is possible, and the possibility of the dice dropping off the table is real as well. The dice works as an example of the heterogeneity of singularity within an event; however, in a sense, it trivializes the conceptual space which Deleuze and Guattari have opened. A more philosophically troublesome example comes from Ludwig Wittgenstein's *Philosophical Investigations*: "If you do not keep the multiplicity of language-games [*Mannigfaltigkeit der Sprachspiele*] in view you will perhaps be inclined to ask questions like: What is a question? – Is it the statement that I do not know such-and-such, or the statement that I wish the other person would tell me … ? – And is the cry 'Help!' such a description?"[21] Wittgenstein finishes his thought with a speculation about the possibilities of transformation and how the multiplicity of the language-games or keeping them organized would, eventually, become clearer in another place. It is contested as to whether or not Wittgenstein ever did make it any clearer. He, as I understand his work, muddled it – and this muddling was to his credit. Just as the throw of the dice "contains" all the possible combinations, so, too, does a Deleuzean event. Wittgenstein's hesitation over the possibilities of transformation corresponds to Deleuze's singularity–event in so far as the phrasing is enmeshed in the action without a direct and knowable cause-and-effect relation:

The problem is therefore one of knowing how the individual would be able to transcend his form and his syntactical link with a world, in order to attain to the universal communication of events [*l'universelle communication des événements*], that is, to the affirmation of a disjunctive synthesis beyond logical contradictions, and even beyond alogical incompatibilities. It would be necessary for the individual to grasp herself as event [*Il faudrait que l'individu se saisisse lui-même comme événement*]; and that she grasp the event actualized within her as another individual grafted [*greffé*] onto her. In this case, she would not understand, want, or represent this event without also understanding and wanting all other events as individuals, and without representing all other individuals as events. Each individual would be like a mirror for the condensation of singularities and each world a distance in the mirror [*chaque monde une distance dans le miroir*].[22]

In the above passage, Deleuze unveils the problem of ethics and politics: ethics and politics are united by and through the Enlightenment (self-present) subject. It is this autonomous individual who, as Kant (the prologue to postmodernity) tells us, is never fully autonomous. It is around the issue of the subject that Deleuze and Kant seem to run similar intellectual paths. Deleuze, however, is bothered, more than is Kant in *The Critique of Pure Reason*, by the belatedness of intelligibility:

Reason concerns itself exclusively with absolute totality in the employment of the concepts of the understanding, and endeavors to carry the synthetic unity, which is thought in the category, up to the completely unconditioned. We may call this unity of appearances the unity of reason,

and that expressed by the category the unity of understanding. Reason accordingly occupies itself solely with the employment of understanding, not indeed in so far as the latter contains the ground of possible experience (for the concept of the absolute totality of conditions is not applicable in any experience, since no experience is unconditioned), but solely in order to prescribe to the understanding its direction towards a certain unity of which it has itself no concept, and in such a manner as to unite all the acts of understanding, in respect to every object, into an absolute whole. I understand by idea a necessary concept of reason to which no corresponding object can be given in sense-experience. … If I speak of an idea, then, as regards its object, viewed as an object of pure understanding, I am saying a great deal, but as regards its relation to the subject, that is, in respect of its actuality under empirical conditions, I am for the same reason saying very little, in that, as being the concept of a maximum, it can never be correspondingly given *in concreto*.[23]

In not having an object in the concrete, or an unalterable syntactical mooring in the world, the subject is left with what Lyotard calls in "Discussions, or Phrasing 'After Auschwitz'" a "paraexperience." It is the Kantian gap between the idea and the concept of reason, or Deleuze's disjunctive synthesis, which makes a determinate experience impossible and, by implication, any cohesive cognition impossible as well. Through Kant and, later, Deleuze a critical force in philosophy is made visible, and that vision, unlike Boethius' vision of Lady Philosophy is incorrigible. The seeing subject, then, is a deconstructed subject living in the wake of postreferential indeterminacy. This decentered subject is the cornerstone of poststructuralist thought, and there is an overabundance of texts annotating the decentered subject's effect on studies in literature, psychoanalysis, and culture. These rehearsals of the

Kantian wound often move toward a quick suturing by way of some banal playfulness of language, or deconstruction as a reading technology. Unlike those weak poststructuralists who are forever increasing the ranks of the unimaginative, Lyotard, like Gilles Deleuze, asks the difficult historico-political question about Auschwitz.

Within a complex poststructuralist or postreferential frame, a frame which I have tried to work in terms of Deleuze's (non)concepts of singularity and event, Lyotard rewrites this historico-political, or modern, moment without its actualization within the unified Enlightenment subject, without its objects being *in concreto*. Instead, Lyotard writes the historico-political as a contest of phrases in and around a *differend*:[24] "The differend is the unstable state and instant of language wherein something which must be able to be put into phrases cannot yet be phrased."[25] It is this rewriting of Auschwitz through the concept of the *differend* that I understand to be Deleuze's intention in speaking of a new type or postreferential revolution in the course of becoming possible.

The *differend* is, I argue, closely allied with Deleuze's concept of singularity–event, in which the instability of language creates a moment of radical doubt within the language-games (genres) of ethics and politics. The referent, that object in the world, hovers above, like the Deleuzean battle, its own ground. This lack of grounding rends the historical fabric by which ethics and politics are arrived at and adjudicated. Perhaps the most crucial event in the twentieth century is Auschwitz. It stands to signify a multitude of ethical and political agendas. For the revisionist historian Faurisson, Auschwitz is the historical event which never was. For others, it is the historical event which will always be. It is this sense of Auschwitz which Lyotard finds so compelling in Adorno. Within a postmodern perspective, Auschwitz always will be an anonym, transcending its status as a place or an historical event:

"Auschwitz" is a model, not an example. From Plato to Hegelian dialectics, the example, says Adorno, has the function in philosophy of illustrating an idea; it does not enter into a necessary relation with what it illustrates, but remains "indifferent" to it. The model, on the other hand, "brings negative dialectics into the real." As a model, "Auschwitz" does not illustrate negative dialectics. Negative dialectics, because it is negative, blurs the figures of the concept (which proceed from affirmation), scrambles the names borne by the stages of the concept in its movement. This model responds to this reversal in the destiny of the dialectic; it is the name of something (of a para-experience, of a paraempiricity) wherein dialectics encounters a non-negatable negative, (*un negatif non niable*), and abides in the impossibility of redoubling that negative into a "result." Wherein the mind's wound is not scarred over. Wherein, writes Derrida, "the investment in death cannot be integrally amortized."

The "Auschwitz" model would designate an experience of language which brings speculative discourse to a halt.[26]

The name "Auschwitz" brings speculative discourse to a halt, first, by denying the Kantian nodal points – a subject who could bear witness[27] to the gas-chamber and the culmination of humanity in an act of consensus about the status of the event – Habermas's project of modernity? Second, the name "Auschwitz" interrupts the synthesis of an understanding, as Adorno indicates, when dialectics encounters a non-negatable negative. Lyotard continues Adorno's point of a non-negatable negative by stating that Auschwitz can no longer be named in the Hegelian sense of naming, "as that figure of memory," like the Deleuzean dice, "which assures the permanence of the *rest* when mind has destroyed its signs."[28]

"Auschwitz" is a name for the anonymous. The collapse of the proper name paired with the extremity of the event opens more fully the anonym "Auschwitz" to another configuration of ethics, politics, subjectivity within the postmodern. The anonym "Auschwitz" bars the litigation over a claim to realism within a cognitive régime. For Lyotard, litigation has ended with the arrival of the *differend*. Instead of competing claims to the real, one has the question: What is to be linked onto Auschwitz?

The question of linkage is the question of justice and, ultimately, the question of the heterogeneity of justice. Claims to the historical real, such as Faurisson's, install an oppressive régime within the universe of phrases. Positivist historians, in a conflict with revisionist historians such as Faurisson, must find the witness he asks for. Both positivist and revisionist historians are tied to realism or unmediated referentiality. In other words, the historians who claim the gas-chamber existed are obligated, because of the cognitive régime, to justify the real experience of the gas-chamber by producing a witness. Revisionist historians need only to ask for the empirical evidence, an eyewitness. Of course, a quick dismissive wave of the hand places Faurisson and those like him in the categories of the insane, the unethical, or the Nazi. But, the question of ethics still persists as a gap between the concept and the Idea of reason. In *The Differend*, Lyotard responds to the cognitive genre by pointing to the silences within it, the multiplicity which has been dialectized:

> That is why the question "Auschwitz?" is also the question "after Auschwitz?" The unchaining of death [*Le déchaînement de l'obligation extrême, la mort*], the utmost obligation, from what legitimates it is perpetuated "after" the crime; scepticism, and even nihilism, have every reason

> to feed off this endlessly. For it is not even true, as Hegel believes, that afterward it still remains for us to chew and digest, in our lair, the "nul and void" of the legitimate linkage [*de l'en-chaînement légitimant*], the extermination of a determined we. The dispersive, merely negative and nearly analytical dialectics at work under the name of "Auschwitz," deprived of its "posi-tive–rational operator," the *Resultat*, cannot engender anything, not even the sceptical we that chomps on the shit of the mind. The name would remain empty, retained along with other names in the network of a world, put into mecanographical or electronic memory. But it would be nobody's memory, about nothing and for no one [*Mais mémoire de personne, à propos de rien et pour personne*].[29]

What does it mean for Auschwitz to be nobody's memory? Lyotard, I think, is assaulting Kant's (here the epilogue to modernity) first nodal point – the knowing subject. In this sense, it is nobody's memory because nobody is capable of synthesizing the singularities and the event. In other words, the gas-chamber is reproducible. The same can be said of the memory being about nothing. To be something is to find an end within the dialectic. Lyotard reads Adorno – correctly, I think – as saying that the end of the dialectic is that novel part of the death camps, that "worse than death."[30]

NAMING DEATH

> (The sea of my memory is white. It will be blue if I want, with words joining in dreams and in the violence of waves swelled and beaten down by fever.

Secret fauna and flora which the reverberations of the page had hidden, now, at the end of the day, I watch them evolve as one might dive with eyes open to explore deep waters.

I go to meet my words and bring them back to the surface, unaware that I lead them to their death.

But this is an illusion.

The surface of the sea is a mirror one breaks in turning the page. All azure of my pen and my death which I importune.

I have the algae for living companions.)

(Edmond Jabès, The Book of Questions)

Are we, then, left with nothing? The answer is yes, if by "nothing" one means a result[31] out of a dialectic; the answer is no, if by "nothing" one means the anonym "Auschwitz" as something which cannot be remembered nor forgotten, a borderland. It is in respect of this tension between not remembering and not forgetting that Lyotard's "paganism" is useful; and it is in *Just Gaming* that he develops it in relation to the ethical–political arena. In *Just Gaming*'s dialogue, Lyotard's interlocutor, Jean-Loup Thebaud, asks: "where does the specificity of paganism lie?"[32] Lyotard answers: "What makes paganism? It consists in the fact that each game[33] is played as such, which implies that it does not give itself as the game of all other games or the true one."[34] A (language-)game that gives itself as the game of all other games is the game of ethics in so far as ethics posits an ontological truth. The same holds true for the (language-)games of politics, Marxism, Freudianism, and feminism. The pagan ends totality by pressing for the invention of new ways of phrasing which can be either actual

86

inventions or alterations of old phrasings. Much like Deleuze's sense of segmentarity, the pagan opens onto the multiplicity of languages with the recognition that *differends* exist and persist. One such *differend* occurs when "Auschwitz" needs to be phrased and cannot yet be phrased. At first one looks to the linkages surrounding the phrasing of "Auschwitz." Whose phrasing is it? The Zionists'?[35] It is the experience of Auschwitz which now serves as the ontological moment of truth. Lyotard asks:

> Why say that this anonym designates an "experience of language," a "para-experience"? Is that not to insult the millions of real dead in the real barracks and gas chambers of real concentration camps? It can be surmised what advantages a well-led indignation can derive from the word reality. And what is spawned by this indignation is the embryo of the justice-maker. It is this indignation, however, with its claim to realism, which insults the name of Auschwitz, for this indignation is itself the only result it derives from that collective murder. It does not even *doubt* that there is a result (namely itself). Now, if this name is a nameless name, if Auschwitz does not provide an example but a mode, it is perhaps because nothing, or at least not all, of what has been expended in it is conserved; because the requirement of a result is therein disappointed and driven to despair; because speculation does not succeed in deriving a profit from it, were it the minimal one of the beautiful soul. That all this is an affair of language is known only too well by asking the indignant ones: what then does "Auschwitz" mean to say to you? For one must, in any case, *speak* [*dire*].[36]

Phrasing since Auschwitz has been a phrasing of the ethical–political from an example or descriptive model. It has urged us to see or glimpse the truth of the gas-chamber when all we are actually able to glimpse is our own "paraexperience." Since we cannot breathe in the gas, we ought not to claim that we can and do. To do so is to speak for those who cannot speak, and this speaking in place of is an annihilation as well. Instead, we have a nameless Auschwitz, an anonym without a moment of translucent intelligibility to be linked ono another event. Auschwitz was and is in the borderland. It is in the borderland now because it works, as Derrida tells us in *The Margins of Philosophy*, as a "breach" (*felure*)[37] – a "unique event, nonreproducible, hence illegible as such and when it happens ... "[38] If Auschwitz is that breach in the ethical–political arena, then what will follow this rupture? This is what Lyotard takes up as an issue of phrasing in "After 'Auschwitz'." Not only is the notion of time, that linear progression of events, breached: the links between these "events" and the constructedness of events themselves are breached. A new type of revolution in the course of becoming possible is not a simple deferral of Auschwitz: it is a revolution which holds open the possibility for an end to oppression, breaching the integrity of the cognitive régime. To not speak for those who cannot speak is to bear witness to their annihilation.

To say, as Faurisson does, "There is, therefore, no gas chamber" is to forge a link between two phrases within an empirical reality. The "there is" suggests an historical reality or referential scheme which serves to measure and adjudicate all links to Auschwitz. Faurisson here points to the unmediated real and calls upon the grand narrative of empiricism to assist in joining a "there is" to a "there is no," with "therefore" serving as the simple hinge. With "therefore," Faurisson instantiates the ready-made frame of empiricism. One then is forced to accept the link "no gas-chamber." A (para)politics out of Deleuze and Lyotard would have us say: "There is therefore ... a differend." The difficulty of a (para)politics is that it calls attention to its own (para)ethical structuration. In other words, unlike the empirical frame

Faurisson invokes, a (para)ethical frame works against itself. It works against itself by acknowledging an "outside" to itself. Outside the frame is the revolutionary point in that the (para)political frame forecloses on its claim to internal integrity and pure referentiality. The gas-chamber, then, was not and is not an enclosed space: it opened and opens on to other points outside of itself which cannot yet be put into phrases. And because of this inability to phrase, as Adorno writes, the death camps take on a "novel horror" – an illegible name, an unmediated silence.

CHAPTER 6

Parasacred ground(ing)s

But age with his stealing steps
Hath clawed me in his clutch,
And hath shipped me into the land,
As if I had never been such.

(Shakespeare, Hamlet)

On the incandescent February morning
Beatriz Viterbo died, after a death
agony so imperious it did not for a
moment descend into sentimentalism or
fear [*despuès de una imperiosa agonía
que no se rebajó un solo instante ni al
sentimentalism ni almedio*], I noticed
that the iron billboards in the Plaza
Constitucion bore new advertisements
for some brand or other of Virginia
tobacco; I was saddened by this fact, for
it made me realize that the incessant
and vast universe was already moving
away from her and that this change was
the first in an infinite series [*el hecho me
dolió, pues comprendí que el incessante y
vasto universo ya se apartaba de ella y que
ese cambio era el primero de una serie
infinita*].

(Jorge Luis Borges, "The Aleph,"
Labyrinths)

ALONGSIDE THE GRAVE

The grave-digger's disquieting song, the
perpetually changing billboards, and the
casual resumption of everyday life, signal
the universe pulling away from the dead
and the living. The vague borders
surrounding life, not exclusively where it
begins and ends, but as it is a lived
moment, around the inevitability of death
itself, fade into an infinite series of
departures and arrivals.

CONSECRATION

The coldness was spreading about as far
as his waist when Socrates uncovered his

face, for he had covered it up and said –
they were his last words – Crito, we
ought to offer a cock to Asclepius. See
to it and don't forget.

(Plato, Phaedo)

Consecrated ground(ing)s come to
express this vague border forming
between the arrival and the departure of
life and death. Consecrated groundings
are parasacred ground(ing)s which are
founded, albeit unsuitably, against that
inevitable fading of the universe in any
number of finitude's disclosures in the
everyday. Grounding the sacred is part of
a bordering and anchoring process that
separates the community of the living
(polis) from the community of the dead
(necropolis). Through the civilizing and
life-affirming conventions of commerce,
law, religion, and the ever-present quiet
practicalities of everyday life (such as
Socrates's final concern), the way to the
community of the dead is tenuously
marked with signs of the ultimate and the
powerful, the parasacred. This vague
border that rises and falls between the
living and the dead, the holy and the
unholy, also can include the sanctified
interstices within a living community that
point more directly to the dead spaces
existing as the internal-negative of the
living. These dead spaces are brought to
consciousness (to life) through the ritual
practices, temples, churches, monuments,
memorials, and architectural structures of
the living for the dead.

These futile (re)cognitions of death, or
bringing death to life, subtly point
outward toward the infinite and also in the
direction of the parasacred, the ultimate
and the powerful in human experience.
There is, in this bringing death to life, an
excess within the sacralizing process; it
is the condition of the sacred which
cannot fully be accommodated in the
space of the living nor the dead. It is for
this reason that sacred ground(ing)s

often exist outside (the pagus) the living habitat, merely bordering the living community. These spaces partially define and aid in giving internal integrity to the living community by statically pointing back from the dead spaces that exist outside and within. They direct the sacred back from the extreme of the exterior and (de)form the negative or reverse image of a living community. These dead spaces surround civilization; they border a city's life and an individual's life. In a similar sense, these sacred ground(ing)s, as anti-life or a paralife, threaten, border, and designate meanings for the living by forcing the expression of *ultimacies* in dead spaces. The graveyard, the absolute terminus, is such a place of ultimate expressions. It is a point of humanity's collective destination and place where the designation of the parasacred is most visible. Moreover, it is the (empty) grave which measures and judges all those proffered ultimacies inscribed in concrete, South African granite, and marble. It renders those inscriptions and engravings (always) inadequate and guilty of a disturbing incompleteness. The power of the graveyard, its sacrality, is its parasacrality – its power to failingly call upon the ultimate. Here, death is found alongside, outside and within.

OUTSIDE–INSIDE FINITUDE

For Jean Baudrillard, in *Symbolic Exchange and Death*, the dead are seen as external to the living, exiled and made into ultimate delinquents who, because of their non-existence, are unretrievable for the living. The unrepatriatable dead, for Baudrillard, are not merely dislocated in death but obliterated into the infinite:

> There is an irreversible evolution from savage societies to our own: little by little, *the dead cease to exist*. They are thrown out of the group's symbolic

circulation. They are no longer beings with a full role to play, worthy partners in exchange, and we make this obvious by exiling them further and further away from the living. In the domestic intimacy of the cemetery, the first grouping remains in the heart of the village or town, becoming the first ghetto, prefiguring every ghetto, but are thrown further and further from the centre towards the periphery, finally having nowhere to go at all, as in the new town or the contemporary metropolis, where there are no longer any provisions for the dead, either in mental or physical space. Even madmen, delinquents and misfits can find a welcome in the new towns, that is, in the rationality of modern society. Only the death-function cannot be programmed and localized. Strictly speaking, we longer no longer know what to do with them, since, today, *it is not normal to be dead*, and this is new. Death is a delinquency, and an incurable deviancy. The dead are no longer inflicted on any place or space or time, they can find no resting place; they are thrown into radical utopia. They are no longer even packed in and shut up, but obliterated.[1]

It is this obliteration of the dead in death that calls attention to an inadequacy and incompleteness of grave expressions which so haunt the interior of the city and the interior of the mortal and finite subject. The grave, in a very real sense, is perpetually open. It is never filled because the grave opens daily, infiltrating the everyday, tearing an opening in the space of the living, creating a dead space that must be and never can be completely filled. These grave expressions around the opening of death appear as engravings and inscriptions, which are always made before the event of obliteration; they attest to the excess of death at the edge of an abyss. It is this excess of death, the open(ing) grave, the abyss, which is the most terrifying obliteration of all. This terror inevitably leads toward the sacred for resolution and solace; and, it is this resounding terror, the feeling of the impending obliteration, which I call the sublime of the parasacred, found before the open(ing) grave that, in the end, founds expressions of ultimacies.

HISTORICIZING THE DEAD

> How does one give oneself death in that other sense in terms of which *se donner la mort* is also to interpret death, to give oneself a representation of it, a figure, a signification or destination for it?
>
> (Jacques Derrida, *The Gift of Death*)

Consecrated grounds represent, figure, signify, and forge the links between the "here" and the "there," life and death. Consecrated grounds bring the "there-ness" of death to the "here-ness" of living. Rural cemeteries – where death is doubly outside – were an American phenomenon of the mid-nineteenth century, often modeled on the available discourses of Romanticism to serve this function of uniting the "here" and "there." American cities of the time achieved their place and stature by having a rural cemetery to offset the encroachment and devastation of urbanization. Such consecrated grounds were intended to provide the dead with a more appropriate resting place, free from overt religiosity, and vandals. The move from the churchyard to a rural setting was also an effect of the fear of contagion. With tuberculosis as the leading cause of death, bodies were better (dis)placed to the outside of the living community. At the same time as the dead were being displaced for health concerns, death itself also underwent a change.

"Cemetery," its Greek origin meaning sleeping chamber, was coined during the

93

Victorian period to replace "graveyard" in the attempt to de-emphasize the finality, horror, and materiality of death. "The cemetery" became the resting- or sleeping-place of the dead, as well as a place of spiritual fulfillment for the living.

Modern cemeteries are descendants of the Greek sleeping chamber in more than name, however. The cemetery is one of very few spaces in postmodern culture to retain a sanctity. As a sanctified place, a cemetery cannot undergo a transformation in the same way a church can become a bookstore, restaurant, or a night club. Cemeteries are dead spaces which cannot be re-converted into a living space. A dead space is the space of the infinite, an infinite which will always defy rehabilitation and reclamation. Sophocles, for instance, depicts the ancient city of Colonus as a space protected by dead-ness, which the terror (the unholy–holy) associated with the grave of Œdipus simultaneously sanctifies and contaminates. Again Baudrillard provides some background to this unholy–holy space which posits death as that which determines the living by attempting to obliterate the dead.

> Death is ultimately nothing more than a social line of demarcation separating the "dead" and the "living": therefore, it affects both equally. Against the sense-less illusion of the living of willing the living to the exclusion of the dead, against the illusion that reduces life to *an absolute surplus-value* by subtracting death from it, the indestructible logic of symbolic exchange re-establishes the equivalence of life and death in the indifferent fatality of survival. In survival, death is repressed; life itself, in accordance with that well known ebbing away, would be nothing more than a survival determined by death.[2]

One finds the sacred articulated in the cemetery in a way that it is not in the graveyard. The sacred disfigures, becoming the parasacred, both holy and unholy, as it stands between the living and the dead. The finality of death also makes for a final instance of exchange, one can argue, that is not determined by gender, race, sexuality, or even the economic. In the last instance, it is death. The grave, the open grave (Figure 6.1) in particular, is the most disturbing of sights/sites in that one is forced to feel the abject dread before (after?) the abyss. It is a place carved out of the earth; it is a gouge; it disturbs, not so much because of what is there as because of what is not – yet. One can view the grave as an aporia, a space not yet designated – the not-yet "filled" condition of the parasacred. This unexpoundable aporia is "defined" by Jacques Derrida in *Aporias* (*Apories: Mourir-s'attendre aux "limites de la vérité"*):

> Let us consider, for example, this negative sentence: "death *has no* border." Or else, let us consider one of these affirmations, which imply something completely different: "death *is* a border," "according to an almost universal figure, death is represented as the crossing of a border, a voyage between here and the beyond, with or without a ferryman, with or without a barge, with or without elevation, toward this or that place beyond the grave." Here, now, is an interrogation: "Can death be reduced to some line crossing, to a departure, to a separation, to a step, and therefore to a *decease*?" And, finally, here is a proposition that could be called interro-denegative: "Is not death, like decease, the crossing of a border, that is a trespassing on death [*un trepas*], an overstepping or a transgression (*transire*, "*sic transit*," etc.)?"
> You have noticed that all these propositions, whatever their modality, involve a certain *pas* [step, not].[3]

Figure 6.1 Open grave

If we are to step after Derrida (Figure 6.2), we must engage in aporetic thinking: we must attempt to think, as he does, the *pas* [step, not]. Perhaps this stepping to and from death could be better illustrated by a return to Œdipus's struggle with and against his own destiny, as both savior and contaminant of Thebes.

The wandering king in *Œdipus at Colonus* attempts the *Il y va d'un certain pas* as he confronts the sacred.

Figure 6.2 Step, not

DEAD STEPS

> "Death is rebellion in the womb of life," Reb Simha went on, "a step

94

accomplished to insert our steps. You
think you walk. You are marking time
on the same spot. Every step forward is
a reptile which, outside time, raises its
head strike."
   (Edmond Jabès, *The Book of Questions*)

Œdipus at Colonus begins with the
violation of a border, a breached limit, a
trespass, a (non)step and an end to
twenty years of wandering. Antigone in
the opening scene of *Œdipus at Colonus*
leads an exhausted Œdipus onto the
consecrated grounds bordering Colonus.
"Holy ground? What god is sacred
here?"[4] Œdipus asks a countryman. It
seems that all the years of wandering
have led him to a place that is the
"untouchable – not to be inhabited";
ironically, it is the very place Œdipus will
ultimately [step, not] and remain. He
acknowledges that he has been "chosen"
to inhabit the uninhabitable: "A sign – my
fate and covenant." What the countryman
cannot fathom is the uncanny return and
metaphysical reversal indicating that
Œdipus actually belongs to the
parasacred, the untouchable, the
uninhabitable, the not. Œdipus, who slew
the Sphinx and brought forth both
civilization and disaster with one blow of
a staff, represents a contradiction within
the sacred. He is, at the same time, holy
and unholy. This sacred, which Œdipus
"represents," is a condition [step, not]
rather than a transcendent place or thing.
It is Œdipus's and humankind's
irreconcilable anxiety that creates the
desire to complete the step, to have a
foothold, to establish, to ground, to
anchor, and to moor an existence. The
anxiety, then, is the impossibility of ever
actualizing that desire because of the
already-openness of the grave. His return
to the untouchable and the uninhabitable,
the " Brazen Threshold," is his return to
the uncanny sacred and the beginning and
culmination of his end – death – the not.

95

For Sophocles, it is Œdipus's
holy–unholy grave which will ultimately
sanctify and protect the city of Colonus.
Ironically, this grave will sanctify and
protect something more than Creon is
able to realize: it is an abyss that
transcends the political moment. The city,
as Sophocles has it, is not founded on
secure ground, but on a fissure, a not:

Ismene: Nevertheless, you ought to
            know that Creon's on his way
            to see if he can use you – and
            sooner now than later.
Œdipus: To use me, daughter? How?
Ismene: To plant you on the frontier of
            Thebes, but not inside:
               Within their reach, of course,
            but not within their sight.
Œdipus: On the threshold, then? What
            use is that?
Ismene: There's a curse upon your tomb
            if it is wronged.
Œdipus: They needed neither god nor
            oracle to tell them that.
Ismene: And so they want to keep you
            somewhere near, not set you up
            in your own right.
Œdipus: Wronged.[5]

What does it mean that Œdipus will be
moored on the frontier, paganized, and
not placed inside the living community?
What kind of death [step, not] is this? It
seems that death for Œdipus is a *pas*
[step, not] in the sense that death for him
is both and simultaneously an arrival and
a departure.
   Œdipus's death is a dying and coming
to life, a return to his origin, destiny, and a
step back and beyond. The seemingly
separate instances in time and place are
brought together in an ironic instance
collected in the act of Œdipus's self-
procreation and death [step, not]. Œdipus
returns to his origin, and, departs toward
death.
   Œdipus attempts to break these
infinite departures and arrivals in his own

death, which is another repetition of his fate. It is Œdipus's death which, for the city of Colonus, seems to bring together arrival and departure, origin and destination. Œdipus's death interferes with and restores this continuity to the community; but, as we learn from Sophocles, there can be no complete restoration of or intimacy with the origin, only a trespass in the return.

Death, especially that described by Sophocles, evokes a vague feeling that allows one to enter into the discourse of "return" or "rebirth." It is the feeling of dread, however, that exceeds, surpasses, and overwhelms the subject. Here, death, as obliteration, overwhelms the sense of "return" or "rebirth." The subject's vague feeling transforms into a feeling of the sublime as it anticipates an obliteration or an annihilation of subjecthood within death. Death infinitely exceeds the human subject and leaves the human subject with a feeling of abject terror. An experience of death is not within chronomatic time because it is not within or contained by consciousness. Hence, Œdipus vanishes into the infinite. The "experience" is ecstatic in so far as the human subject is exceeded by the non-concept of the infinite. The terror, then, is terror without an object (grave) or a subject (consciousness). In this formulation, the anxious moment of death is a moment in time that anticipates a breach of the limits of consciousness and finitude. The movement from time to outside time, from finitude to infinity, is one marked by the subject seeing its own limits within extreme anxiety, where the condition for all things being possible is imagined. It is in that particular moment one finds the grave, the aporia, as it pressures consciousness to "feel" its own limits as the sublime. Described by Jean-François Lyotard, it is a moment when "[t]hought feels its moorings in the sensory being ripped away and its object trembling at the edge of the abyss."[6] The

grave, as aporia, is in excess of consciousness, and it is the sacred that has traditionally functioned to represent the unpresentable. The irony is that ascribing to something the value of the sacred, naming the infinite, raises the specter of the dialectic. In this moment, the naming of the infinite does not solve the problem of excess – it causes it. At what point does the infinite surpass the finite? In other words, how does the infinite differ from the finite? One can recall that this was Zeno's predicament – what separates here from there?

DEAD SPACE

The grave, the aporia, and the para-phernalia that surrounds it, illustrate this tension between the here and the there. The grave marker points to the there from the here; Or, one could ask, does it point to the here from the there? The here and the there, from either direction, meet at the site of the grave. The grave itself is a negative moment in that one sees the surrounding ground, the marker, in order to see the (w)hole, the nothing. It is the empty space or the not-space, the dead space which cannot be represented, only alluded to in a variety of ritualistic practices.

Like Zeno, the mourners are left with yet another not-space to be divided and divided yet again. The not-space is perpetually infinite in its (non)presence. Is the "not here" necessarily the "there," as the marker would suggest? Is the "not there" necessarily "here"? The not-space does not necessarily function dialectically or reciprocally. The difference between the two cannot be determined by degrees, only by a kind of radical, terror-filled, singularity. Here and there are not linked within a continuum. Here and there are not dialectically intertwined with one fading into the other. Ultimate (religious) experiences are brought into conjunction with this movement of consciousness. Human consciousness perpetually bears the weight of death and thus alternates between attraction and repulsion. With this sense of anxiety still in mind, exploring the parasacred is the probing and marking of the (dead) spaces in which anxiety occurs around ultimacy. Where do these eruptions of the terrifying take place and where do they reside in human consciousness? These eruptions, I propose, take place in the "graveyard" (the place of the dead without rest) itself and on the markers that stand to perpetuate completeness and defer fragmentation. These eruptions take place, I propose, at the limits of human consciousness. In effect, these terrifying moments never take place as such. Instead, they are terrifying in that they do not take place within consciousness; they exceed human consciousness, and this is what is terrifying.

If the notion is at all true that the grave is the final resting-place in so far as it marks a closure, a filling-in, a covering-over, it should be easily tested by the degree of restfulness one finds there. And although this is the common wisdom, I argue against it – the grave is not a place of rest: it is a place of memory, sorrow, longing, and Otherness. Grave sites are unsteady points along an infinite series of abysses. Graves, in a manner of speaking, speak out or call out or hold the grave contents within the ground. Grave sites mark the surface, and attempt to fill the aporia with meaning.

What follows is a grave study.

PARASACRED ERUPTIONS

The Welch grave marker (Figure 6.3) depicts a gesturing hand, a finger pointing upward. Is it pointing to heaven, to God? The intention of the pointing is not altogether clear. Is it merely a

fashionable pointing, a style of grave marker? Is it a prescriptive pointing? Does the hand instruct us to attend to heaven or to an ultimate concern? Is it a stern hand commanding our attention to the "above?" Is it a hand that judges us? Whose hand is it? Is it Welch's hand? Is Welch warning us from beyond the grave? Is Welch indicating where he is, now? Is it a soothing hand telling us not to worry about him, for he is in heaven? What is at hand?

Figure 6.3 Welch

The supplicant hands (Figure 6.4) are less ambiguous than the directional hand of the Welch grave marker. The viewer is

Figure 6.4 Supplicant hands

able to choose from a range of possible interpretations, beginning with the question: Whose hands are they? In the overtly religious sense, they are the hands of Jesus praying for the deceased. By extension they are simply the praying hands of a saint or church appointee. It is the question of prayerfulness that seems to disturb the next level of interpretation: Are the hands simply praying to God? Are they thankful hands? Petitioning hands? Penitent hands? In the context of the cemetery, the hands offer eternal prayer for the dead. The hands statically "pray" in the absence of mourners. The hands, then, substitute for the grieving visitors into eternity. Supplicant hands links the here-and-there in non-linear time. The grave marker addresses the infinite need of prayer and the finitude of loss.

Figure 6.5 depicts one hand descending from the clouds and two hands reaching up, but not quite touching the "offered" hand. TAKE MY HAND is not strictly an offering: it is a request. The hands are not alone and separate (Welch), nor are they together (the supplicant hands): they are active hands, reaching hands. They are hands in need of the Lord's hand, in need of lifting. It is just, merely, only the hands that communicate the anxiety over salvation. The hands are a synecdoche for humanity and for God. The Lord's hand breaks through the clouds to retrieve the hands of the person, to lift the deceased into heaven.

In the crucifixion, Christianity is held in suspension. The life-sized figures of the crucified Jesus and the attendants (Figure 6.6) mark the grave as a site qualified or conditioned by the suffering on the cross, the death of God.

The grave marker as historico-theological re-enactment cites the second most powerful scene from Christian history as a reminder of Jesus's suffering, or that death will be overcome by Jesus – or death will overcome Jesus. The crucifixion re-enactment is "postmodern"

Figure 6.5 Hands reaching

as it perpetually presents itself and, in the eternal presentation, eclipses and postpones the single most important event within the Christian narrative, the resurrection. The "post" of christianity is the crucifixion or Christianity before it realized its *rule*, the resurrection. The crucifixion scene has its power of

Figure 6.6 Crucifixion

representation of ultimacy only through an implied sacrality, a "para"-sacrality, and, here, within the deferred resurrection of Jesus, the overtly religious grave marker depends upon one point in the narrative structure which, revealing and containing the entire structure, totalizes the narrative. Therefore, the crucifixion must and can only imply the resurrection in such as way as to suggest that the narrative events are always remaindered or deferred to another event within the entire narrative structure. Does the crucifixion unequivocally answer the terror of death? Are the viewers from the roadside who pass it on their way to their destinations supposed to see the marker as a reminder of God's promise or a remainder within God's promise – the deferral of resurrection – or the death of God.

Death, as it is portrayed within the overtly religious grave markers, is a kind of waiting for something destined to arrive, a waiting during which nothing seems to arrive because of the postponement. The reminder of the crucifixion is one of extreme sacrifice while the remainder is one of perpetually deferment. The massive structure stands out from among the more modest and conventional grave markers which fit into neat rows perpendicular to a country road. The lighted scene of the crucifixion seems out of place on top of a hill just yards from a weathered barn and house. At night the scene is illuminated by floodlights and can be seen from afar. The death of God takes place among the common surroundings of central New York State. How is one to read the contrast? As a reminder to be more appreciative of Jesus's sacrifice? As a pointing to a remainder or an excess within theology? The crucifixion scene titles the cemetery in its prescription of faith, or its deferral of salvation, or the impossibility, through the death of God, of either.

The choices and selections to be made

concerning the overtly religious or dedicational grave markers are extensive in range. One can choose an historical re-enactment of the crucifixion or one can select from a number of minor religious figures and themes. The Virgin Mary in Figure 6.7 is a devotional marker that is a subsidiary of the God-related markers. "Hail Mary ... full of grace. The Lord is with thee ... " begins the prayer to her as a para-deity.

Mary's presence is different from her presence beneath the crucified Christ. She is in post-assumption and, hence, is more inviting and, by implication, more

Figure 6.7 Hail Mary

religious. Mary's presence as a minor deity and not just a witness to the crucifixion places a gap between her person and God by establishing her function as that either of an emissary of God or of an advocate for humanity. Her status is and has always been ambiguous within Christian theology, and this occupation of the parasacred further defers the promise of the resurrection and complicates her role within the heavenly order. Hail Mary presents Mary as humanity's advocate within God's design. Mary's own assumption (not ascension) into heaven becomes a model or precedent for the decedent. Sacrality is expressed as parasacrality in Hail Mary to the extent that Mary is not God, but around God. The light-rays beaming behind her place her outside of the center, on the periphery of, or within the para of the sacred, heaven. Mary's prayerful repose suggests that she is interceding on the behalf of humanity until or instead of the resurrection.

Unlike Hail Mary, in which she advocates for humanity, the Emanating Mary (Figure 6.8) marker is active. Instead of God's light illuminating her from above, Mary seems to have her own light, her own illumination. The engraving, in which Mary is depicted in her traditional blue garment and white veil, does in fact portray Mary as more assertive, if not actually autonomous.

Mary, as autonomous, also is a part of another tradition which substitutes God's powers in favor of Mary's powers. The pop-rendering raises Mary to the level of cult figure with god-like powers of healing and forgiveness. In this sense, Mary is part of the pagan sacred – a system of substitutions and reversals of standard Christian theology.

The traditional image of Mary, Mother of God (Figure 6.9), returns Mary to the subsidiary role of advocate. Mary passively holding the active Jesus (he

Figure 6.8 Emanating Mary

100

gestures) is consistent with Christian tradition.

Nevertheless, Mary plays a part in defining and shaping what is powerful and ultimate in Christianity. She presents Jesus to the world in his infancy, and it is

Figure 6.9 Mary, Mother of God

his infancy that elevates her role in the religious order. Mary, Mother of God, however, seems to mis-state the actual theological relationship that exists between Mary and God. Mary is the mother of Jesus, the infant. She is a witness to the crucifixion who is assumed into heaven by God. It is clear that she does not have power independent of God. Mary's place within the sacred order continually shifts from center to periphery, as Jesus moves from infancy to adulthood.

John the Baptist (Figure 6.10) is also a parasacred figure in terms of grave markers. While Mary seems occasionally to substitute for God, John the Baptist occasionally substitutes for Jesus.

This act of substitution is carefully monitored in the engraving, in which the image of Jesus is etched into John the Baptist's image. Clearly, the religious figures all point toward a Christian vision of ultimacy. However, within that vision, the subsidiary figures are aberrations or, at least, qualifications of the sacred. Religious figures all point to God the Father eventually. It is within the spaces along the way to the eventual concentration of sacrality in God that one sees the distortions of sacrality as parasacrality. The saints, Mary, and Jesus all enter into a play of figures, much like a play of signs with a transcendent referent. All the figures, it is assumed, point back to their origin and destination. In moments of parasacrality, however, the figures often point in other directions. This pointing back is incomplete and subject to deviation.

There is a difference between grave markers when one considers whether or not the articulation/gesture (the marking) is a pointing to or a filling of the aporia. The religious markers shown here are articulations which to some degree attempt to fill the aporia. The articulation is not merely a gesture in so far as the articulation is one of hope and/or

Figure 6.10 John the Baptist

speculation. There are other markings which are gestures, gestures without hope and/or speculation. They leave the aporia as an aporia, unfilled. One could argue that such markers (which are discussed in Chapter 7) intercede on behalf of the aporia against hope and/or speculation. These markers are parasacred in that they defer the totalization of the ultimate and posit their own minor ultimacies – football and fishing. These minor ultimacies must first draw our attention to the aporia itself by "drawing" us into the grave.

As we become an audience for and of the dead we are reminded that cemeteries are "postmodern" to the extent that chronomatic time is placed under arrest, paused and held in the custody of figural time. While cemeteries are heavily inscribed with indicators of chronomatic time – date of birth, date of death, date of marriage – they remain a site in which "time," that "time" we measure and experience, ceases to be a constant.

As one walks through a cemetery, time transforms into a no-thing, an immeasurable aporia, and our own place as audience transforms into that of performer, a performer of time (Figure 6.11). The nothing, the aporia, comes in between the dates to mark the time of life. The aporia "appears" also as a marked absence, as the dash or gash. Time is the dash/gash in between the dates inscribed for birth and death (Figure 6.12).

What does it mean to see "time," one's life or another's life, as a dash/gash, a lifetime as a dash/gash/[–]? In one sense, this "time" is both finite and infinite. The dash can be shortened to 12:00 pm June 11, 1879 dash/gash/[–]9:00 am February 10, 1968. The [–] is shorter in that it shaves hours from the [–]. What if one were to add seconds to the hours and minutes? 12:00:01[–]9:00:05. Or hundredths or thousandths of seconds? Would not the [–] eventually shorten, infinitely? Chronomatic time expands in its contraction as the dash/gash/[–] lengthens by shortening.

The grave markers reveal other time inscriptions which attempt to give meaning to the infinite [–]. Where does one find the lifetime in the [–]? To begin, the en*gravings* which are a standard feature of (Christian) grave markers function to qualify the [–] by further lengthening or shortening the [–]. Psalm 23 (Figure 6.13), for instance, fills the empty space between the dates only partially.

The young woman chained to an anchor (Figure 6.14) is one of a pair standing either side of a grave. She lifts her eyes up to heaven. Her mortal remains and the anchor are linked in opposition to her spirit, which seeks the heavenly. As she longingly gazes to the heavens, her anchor grounds her, her body stands in the way of her fulfillment in the hereafter.

The anchor alone (Figure 6.15a) and the

Figure 6.11 Dates

Figure 6.12 Dash

Figure 6.13 Psalm 23

figure clinging to the cross (Figure 6.15b) depict the ambiguity of the anchor as an image. While the anchor denotes the body and the imprisonment of the spirit in the body, it functions also as something which grounds in a much different sense. The cross is the anchor that the figure uses to ground or fix his or her place in the sacred order. The anchor–cross is a substitution of grounds. The body anchors the spirit negatively and the cross (as a symbol) anchors the spirit positively on sacred grounds.

The second anchored figure (Figure 6.16), the disfigured twin of the first (6.14), mimics the latter's pose from the opposite side of the grave. Her body, too, is chained to an anchor, and the anchor becomes a metaphor for the body and, subsequently, for mortality and finitude. Her gaze also is fixed on the heavens. The longing for the heavenly, however, sets mortality against immortality, as in the earlier figure but with an exception: her longing seems more desperate, her redemption less assured.

The anguish of the figure clinging to the cross and of the vandalized figure is set against the seeming contentment of the young woman in Figure 6.14.

The cemetery is that uneasy transitional space of the living and the dead. The anguished figures reveal the mortal moment of anxiety when life and death meet. The figures are in transition from the body to the spirit, and neither expression – contentment, anguish – seems adequate to the resolution of the perpetual liminality here presented. The parasacrality of the cemetery emerges within this inadequacy as an aporia and an anguish over the step, the transition to the beyond. What will fill death? What will come in place of the anchor? Another anchor? The cemetery is an expression of this anxiety-producing aporia as more and more figurations come to challenge the grave.

103

Figure 6.14 Anchored figure

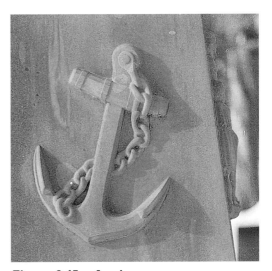

Figure 6.15a Anchor

Figure 6.15b Clinging to the Cross

104

Figure 6.16 Twin anchored figure

CHAPTER 7

Paragrave

To think not is to linger with a negative, which, though it can never be negated, is not merely negative. The not is something like a non-negative that nonetheless is not positive. So understood, the not does not exist; nor does the not exist. Neither something nor nothing, the not falls *between* being and nonbeing.

(Mark C. Taylor, *Nots*)

Contrary to my usual custom I had come into the garden which is called the garden of the dead, where again the visitor's farewell is rendered doubly difficult, since it is meaningless to say: yet once more, when the last time is already past, and since there is no reason for ceasing to say farewell, when the beginning is made after the last time is past. Most of the visitors had already gone home, only an individual here and there vanished among the trees; not glad to meet anyone, he avoided the contact, seeking the dead not the living. And always in this garden there prevails a beautiful understanding among visitors, that one does not come here to see and to be seen, but each visitor avoids the other.

(Søren Kierkegaard, *Concluding Unscientific Postscript*)

ULTIMATE ANXIETY

Where one finds expressions of ultimate concern, one also finds expressions of ultimate anxiety. Kierkegaard's "garden of the dead" becomes the canvas upon which human subjectivity is rendered. In *Concluding Unscientific Postscript*, the contest between ultimate concern and ultimate anxiety comes into focus around issues of subjectivity, representation, speculative philosophy, and faith.

Kierkegaard writes of a walk in the cemetery, to which he was unaccustomed, and of his overhearing an old man asking, perhaps begging, his grandson to forswear speculation. For Kierkegaard this plea, made near the new grave of his son, the boy's father, pulls at the limits of the witness to truth in Christianity. The son–father died, the grandfather says, not "in faith" but believing rather in the kind of speculation which leads to representation. The grandfather's solace (his ultimate concern) becomes his fear (ultimate anxiety) as he considers the son's–father's error in turning away from the acknowledgement

> that there was one name in which alone there was salvation, the name of the Lord Jesus Christ. He ceased speaking for a moment, and then said half aloud to himself: "That this solace should have become my fear, that he, my son, now buried there in the grave, should have relinquished it. To what end then all my hope, my care, to what end his wisdom, when as now his death in the midst of his error must make a believer's soul uncertain of his salvation, must bring my gray hairs in sorrow to the grave, must cause a believer to leave the world in anxiety, an old man to hasten like a doubter after certainty, and to look despondently about him upon those he leaves behind!"[1]

This contemplation of salvation that takes place in the graveyard has two opposed limits: the question of what is left behind after death; and the question of what is ahead after life. The tension is brought to an extreme by involving the contemplative subject who imagines his or her own death and what that death comes to mean, ultimately.

The space of and for the *dead*, the graveyard, is actually a collection of tensions involving faith and speculation. As we saw in the previous chapter, the image of the hands on the grave markers ambiguously directs our attention "above" to God(?), while the Virgin Mary and John the Baptist direct our attention more to the attendant religious figures who will, the supplicant hopes, relay prayers and concerns to God. Kierkegaard's point in "Truth is Subjectivity" is that the graveyard needs to be iconoclastic space. Faith is set against speculation in so far as faith refuses to give a name or figure to the beyond. The grave should be left unfilled if it is to give meaning to death.

Anchored meaning in an iconoclastic graveyard is an impossibility. It is only through human finitude and the inadequacy of representation in relation to the infinite that another meaning becomes available. The grave is most meaningful when it is irreverent, unmarked, or marked as being overwhelming and not susceptible to totalization. It is in this sense that the subject approaches the grave or steps toward the grave with ultimate anxiety as the ultimate concern.

Figure 7.1 Contemplation, not thinking

about death. While she shares with the grandfather a general anxiety, her anxiety differs in so far as it is Kierkegaard's anxiety, an anxiety linked to the question of knowing the condition of "salvation," but not sharing in it.

108

PARADEATH

The contemplative figure marking Walch's grave (Figure 7.1) sits with her chin resting on her right hand. The direction of her gaze is indeterminate: her eyes are fixed neither on the heavens nor on the earth. Her study is not a self-study. It is study of the tension between what is left behind after death and what lies ahead after life. There is no religious symbol or icon guiding her thoughts, nor a biblical phrase promising her, or her viewers, redemption. Nothing, save the infinite liminality, encloses her gaze. Instead of waiting for redemption, she sits alongside two spaces and remains perpetually paralocated between the twin anxieties of knowing and anticipating. It is the contemplative figure that best approximates Kierkegaard's own anxiety

ANCHORS

Just as the contemplative figure is paralocated in relation to what one leaves behind before death and what lies ahead after death, the anchored figures, too, draw our attention to this anxiety. The raised figure (Figure 7.2) fixes her gaze upward to a non-disclosed place above the horizon. While one may assume that the grave is a Christian grave, one should not assume the importance of that belief to death. There is absent from the figure any linkage to Christianity. The figure's eyes look upward at the same time the anchor holds her to the ground. This anchored figure, like the contemplative figure, is caught in a tension between the here and there. Neither place comes to explicit articulation outside of the gaze and the symbolic weight of the anchor.

> Nor does one need the company, least of all a gossipy friend, here where all is eloquence, where the dead man calls out the brief word engraved upon his tombstone. He does not expound and expand like a clergyman, but is like a silent man who says only this one word, but says it with a passion as if to burst the tomb – or is it not strange to have inscribed upon his tombstone: "We shall meet again"; and then to remain in the grave?
>
> (Søren Kierkegaard, *Concluding Unscientific Postscript*)

In the age of postmodernism, in which meaning and value are diverse and unanchored, the car replaces the crucifix as a parasacred symbol (Figure 7.3). The car does not directly invoke the grave anxiety found in the "contemplative" figure or the "anchored" figures. Instead, the car is almost completely areligious in so far as it does not readily draw our attention to the tension, the gap, between the here and the there as one may understand it. While it is true that our attention is not at the command of a specific anxiety (here/there), it is at the command of an anxiety nonetheless. If one takes the grave as that moment which calls upon the subject to cry out his or her ultimate concern, then the car is perhaps the most anxious cry of all. Unlike the Holy Cross, the Virgin Mary, an angel or other religious image, the car cries out an ultimacy without resolution and without promise. There is no redemption or salvation in the car: it offers no solace; nor does it offer fear. What is does offer is parasacrality. It offers ultimacy before the rule of the ultimate. It offers salvation and redemption as a pagan ultimacy – before the sacred became sacred and the center. Like any graven image, the car is

109

Figure 7.2 Raised figure, anchored

irreverently pious in that it defers "Ultimacy" for "ultimacies." The car respects these "ultimacies" or the infinite by not naming them and by not totalizing

Figure 7.3 Car

them within a narrative of salvation. The car opens the "Ultimate" to the "plural ultimate" by way of the "para" which is always alongside, beside, and a subsidiary of the sacred. In this sense, the irreverent/iconoclastic "car" is more pious than the overtly religious as it parodies and speaks directly of the inadequacy of the representation(s) of the aporia.

The football player (Figure 7.4) and the fisherman (Figure 7.5) appear alongside one another on a dark granite marker. The marker indicates two graves, a husband and wife, yet it is filled with predominantly sporting images. Unlike other shared headstones that celebrate a love transcending death, this shared text lifts football and fishing to the heights of ultimacy. It is the substitution of football and fishing for romantic love which first sets apart the shared headstone from the everlasting marriage motif. One could understand a substitution if it were one of religious conviction, for instance, the everlasting marriage motif giving way to standard religious scene of the crucifixion or the appearance of the Virgin Mary. This, however, is not the case. The football player and the fisherman stand closer to ultimacy than either the everlasting marriage or religious conviction. What is it, then, that makes the football player and the fisherman suitable articulations of the powerful and the ultimate in human existence? Is it just an irreverence? Or, is it a deeper sense of faith? If the grave cannot be filled by the promise of salvation or a simple belief in God, then why not offer a football player or a fisherman? If any and all representations are, in the end, inadequate, what makes a football player or fisherman less appropriate than Jesus Christ, the Virgin Mary, or John the Baptist? In faith, the football player and the fisherman speak more directly to the excess of the grave and the excess of death. The two images are insufficient offerings in that all

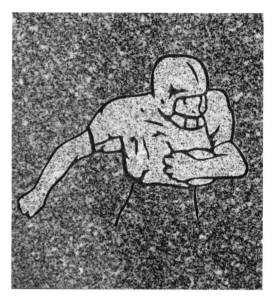

Figure 7.4 Football player

Figure 7.5 Fisherman

offerings are insufficient – death exceeds all gestures toward completion.

If we understand the postmodern to mean that which comes before the establishing of the rule, then the parasacred is the pre-arrival of the sacred in the age of postmodernism. The irreverence of the "car," the "football player," the "fisherman," are instances of irreverent piety in so far as each rendering defers to name the ultimate as the Ultimate. The "car" is postmodern, that is para, in the way it refuses to link to a metanarrative such as Christianity. Ultimacy is expressed as a radical heterogeneity specific only to the subject addressing the sacred. The "car" speaks for nothing but itself, and, even then the speaking is radically singular. This paralogy is a perpetual anterior instance which disallows linkages or metanarratives (regarding the human, art, religion, literature). Linkages are contingent, arbitrary, and not forged to anything other than another singularity. To the extent that any singularity is linked to another, its link is unnecessary; it can be, perhaps should be, reinvented from the beginning.

The Christian pyramid (Figure 7.6), Egyptian revival architecture, is a search for a beginning. The pyramid holds the cross high above the cemetery as if the two were one piece. They are not. The pyramid is of granite blocks and the cross is of limestone. The two are joined or fastened together by an iron pin. In another context, the pyramid and the cross are separate pieces at a more profound level.

The Egyptian sense of immortality is not the Christian sense of immortality. Although the Greek concept of the soul derives from an Egyptian source, everlasting life is conditioned by the acceptance of the crucifixion and resurrection of Jesus Christ, while the Egyptian is conditioned by the continuum of life.

D.H. Lawrence's novella *The Man Who Died* marks the incompatibility, and then the compatibility, of Egyptian mythology and Christian theology through the complexity of the return. It is the man who dies who awakes to the body: the resurrection is the erection. The man who dies meets the priestess and a pagan

Figure 7.6 Christian pyramid

christianity, a drifting christianity, is

formed.

> "Art thou not that slave who possessed the maiden under the eyes of Isis? Art thou not the youth? Speak!"
>
> The youth stood up in the boat in terror. His movement sent the boat bumping against the rock. The slave sprang out in wild fear, and fled up the rocks. The man who died quickly seized the boat and stepped in, and pushed off. The oars were yet warm with the unpleasant warmth of the hands of a slave. But the man pulled slowly out, to get the current which set him down the coast, and would carry him in silence. The high coast was utterly dark against the starry night. There was no glimmer from the peninsula: the priestess came no more at night. The man who died rowed slowly on, with the current, and laughed to himself: "I have sowed the seed of my life and my resurrection, and put my touch forever upon the choice woman of this day, and I carry her

perfume in my flesh like essence of roses. She is dear to me in the middle of my being. But the gold and flowing serpent is coiling up again, to sleep at the root of my tree. So let the boat carry me. Tomorrow is another day."[2]

Osiris returns to join with Isis, and the lion, of course, returns to the Sphinx, to the beginning again. The presence of the return in the cemetery reminds the visitor that he or she is not a visitor, but a future occupant. The Sphinx has a secret, and it is the terror of death. Beginning is ending, ending is beginning and finitude expresses its parasacrality in between those twin terrors waiting for the return of death.

CHAPTER 8

Epilogue

Paraultimacy

Postmodern parainquiry, with its emphasis on liminality, also presents to us an inaccessible space arising not before death or after life, but in between and alongside life *and* death. In the cemetery, the visitor finds himself or herself pulled by a certain anxiety toward this infinite space. The visitor at first desires to leave the space of the cemetery, to step back from it into another, more comfortable, space of the living. The visitor then, out of a competing desire, steps forward into the space of the dead (Figure 8.1).

The cemetery invites one to struggle with the tension of stepping back and stepping forward and it is in this struggle, this anxiety, that one realizes that the two steps are not exclusive of one another, nor do they follow one another. To step back is to step forward into the space of the living. It is to step forward into one's life, thus deferring the grave. To step forward is to step back, to step into contemplation (Figure 8.2).

To step forward is to step back into the anxiety between the here-and-the-there. Stepping forward into the space of the dead disrupts the continuity of the stepping back and forward into one's life. Stepping forward and stepping back folds time over onto itself. Beginning and ending appear to be tied together by a dash or a cut. It is this small mark that indicates a lifetime, a lifetime that in the cemetery is conditioned by the constant opening of the grave.

Stepping forward as a stepping back into the contemplation of the here-and-the-there presses upon consciousness to consider the infinite space of the *para*. The visitor, now future occupant of the grave, must actively think of his or her death. The visitor–future occupant must think of his or her own obliteration within the infinite of the *para*.

115

Figure 8.1 Steps, corridor

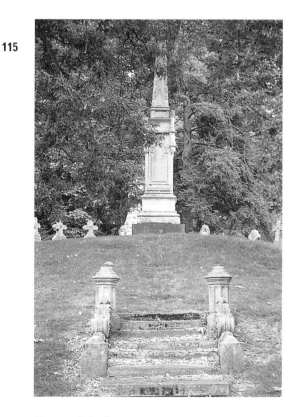

Figure 8.2 Steps

The steps, the corridor, to the plot lift the visitor–future occupant toward the "there." The steps ascend, the walls contain, and the subject who begins in the "here" arrives at the final step and the "there." But the "there" is not a place; it is not a space. It is nothing. The subject arrives before the no-place clutching a cross, a fishing rod (the rood), a football, and the no-place does not yield. The cross, the fishing rod (the rood), the football, all fall into the grave leaving it unfilled. The grave always remains unfilled and unsettled.

> "Nail down the Lid": Listen to the cry of a woman in labor at the hour of giving birth – look at the dying man's struggle at his last extremity – and then tell me whether something that begins and ends thus could be intended for enjoyment.
>
> True, we humans do everything possible to get away as quickly as possible from those two points; we hurry as much as possible to forget the cry of birth-pangs and to change into the pleasure the act of having given life to another being, And when someone is dead we hasten to say: He went to sleep gently and softly; death is sleep, a quiet sleep – all of which we do not proffer for the sake of the deceased, since our words cannot help him in the slightest, but for our own sakes, so as not to lose our joy in life; we do it in order to have everything serve to heighten our joy in life during the interim between the birth-cry and the death-cry, between the mother's cry and the child's repetition thereof in the hour of death.[1]

POSTMODERN ANXIETY

Postmodernism is not a philosophy of pure despair or pure hope. Does the

116   **Figure 8.3 Angel out of stone**

Angel of Death lead us from the "Here" toward the "There" (Figure 8.3)? Previously, the sacred filled the grave for us in the way Jesus Christ, for Christians, overcame death in the resurrection. Today we have no such sacred and no such angel to lead us out of the "Here" to the "There." Instead, there is merely the *para* that does not fill the grave and the paratheological that does not console the living, the dying, and the dead with its absence of a concrete promise of redemption. The *para* stands alongside the anxiety of postmodernism unable to dissipate it or settle it. For those who view postmodernism as the newest "new" form of literary criticism, eclecticism, pluralism, and neo-liberalism have overlooked its terrible consequence: death without redemption. Postmodernism is like a very good solvent. It cleaned current academic ventures of the old paradigm. It seemed to breathe new life into gasping paradigms, abandoned tired tropes, and updated lexicons. Taken together, all of these enterprises, too, dissolve. One cannot remove a foundation in the name of anti-foundationism only to re-instate a foundation that is more pleasing to an array of ideological formations or neurotic styles. The paraethical, the parasacred, the paraphilosophical are the no steps, neither "Here" nor "There," that characterize the condition of our age. Parainquiry in the age of postmodernism leaves us unable to think and live comfortably, with either the simple presence or absence of an ultimate concern. We are forever posed alongside the angel (Figure 8.4): we are, today, intermediate creatures without foundation, left vandalized between a "here" that is inexhaustible and a "there" that is not.

117

Figure 8.4 Postmodern angel

GLOSSARY

I should say that in so far as they are bees, they don't differ from one another.

(Plato, Meno)

But there is one thing you must do. If you want to be thoroughly exercised, you must not merely make the supposition that such and such a thing *is* and then consider the consequences; you must also take the supposition that the same thing *is not*.

(Plato, Parmenides)

[T]he real is not only that which can be reproduced, but that which is already reproduced, the hyperreal, which is entirely simulation.

(Jean Baudrillard, Simulations)

There are twenty types of definition[1]: (1) circular; (2) connotative; (3) contextual; (4)

denotative; (5) essence; (6) functional; (7) *genus et differentia*; (8) historical; (9) lexical; (10) loaded; (11) nominal; (12) operational; (13) ostensive; (14) persuasive; (15) precising; (16) real; (17) recursive; (18) stipulative; (19) synonymous; (20) syntactical. Accompanying the twenty types of definition are thirteen "rules for defining": (1) a definition must indicate the essential characteristics of the thing being defined; (2) the definition should give the *genus and differentia* of the thing being defined; (3) the *definiendum* should not appear in the *definiens*; (4) the *definiens* should be more clear than the *definiendum*; (5) the *definiendum* must be synonymous with the *definiens*; (6) a definition should be precise; (7) a definition should be concise; (8) a definition should not be ambiguous; (9) a definition should be easily understood; (10) a definition should not be vague; (11) a definition should not be expressed in metaphors or figurative language; (12) a definition must not be defined in negatives, *via negativa*; (13) a definition must not be stated in opposite and correlative terms.[2]

Alterity Nondiscursive and radical otherness present within language. Non-negotiable difference.

Anxiety The free-floating specificity of the infinite contained within events and expressed as the finitude of human subjectivity. Also: maximal extremity of intelligibility.

Aporia An opening in language and experience that is not reducible to language or experience. Also: a rupturing of intelligibility.

Death The feeling and/or thinking of radical otherness that is not confinable within language, but nevertheless is represented graphically within the symbolic order.

Differend   *Le différend* is a term coined by the French philosopher Jean-François Lyotard (1924–1998) to describe the incommensurabilty of language-games and the absence of the objective rendering of thought in discourse. His book entitled *The Differend* is a study of the notion of incommensurability in the history of philosophy.

Event   The once and singular linking of phrases within temporality and the totality of phrases comprising the universe.

Immemorial   The limit of consciousness within the temporal.

Language-games   *Les jeux de langage* (Lyotard) and *Sprachespiele* (Wittgenstein) are terms that denote the context-dependent ordering of signs which enable (mis)communication. Meaning derives from the assembling of rules governing the use of words.

Para   The non-negatable image of a concept.

Paraethics   The condition by which universal moral principles are deferred by the singularity of phrases. Also: the expression of moral urgency around the multiplicity of language-games and the heterological structuration of the universe of phrases.

Parasacrality   The ultimate without centrality, distributed throughout the totality of phrases that

comprise the universe. Also: the unpresentable maximal intensity of supreme value within human existence – Yahweh, Jesus Christ, sports cars, golf, planes, boats, the crucifix, etc.

Postmodernism   "Postmodernism" is used to describe a wide spectrum of aesthetic, cultural, historical, literary, and philosophical endeavors. It is often also used to signify, variously, an eclectic style, an historical period, and a philosophical concept, as well as an anti-style, an atemporal event, and a non-concept. Often associated with deconstruction and poststructuralism, it is a term whose reference is in a process of perpetual redefinition.

In the visual arts and in architecture, postmodernism is taken to mean pastiche or eclecticism. In philosophy, postmodernism's defining features are its divestment of logocentrism and its conceptual dismantling of the quest for epistemological certainty that has characterized Western philosophy since Descartes. Postmodern philosophy is anti-foundational, and sometimes is viewed as contemporary skepticism.

In the 1960s, French philosophers such as Roland Barthes, Gilles Deleuze, Jacques Derrida, Michel Foucault, and Jean-François Lyotard departed from conventional studies in the history of philosophy and began to address the epistemological crisis underpinning Western philosophical thought. Their early scholarship focused on the structure of language and its role in forming world-views. The work of the Swiss linguist Ferdinand de Saussure, especially his posthumous text entitled *Course in General Linguistics*, presented the intellectual insight that was necessary in order to separate the synchronic and diachronic elements of language. Dividing language and, in effect, freeing the sign from the signified, permitted poststructuralists to redefine language as a system of differential signs.

The early writings of the French philosopher Jacques Derrida complicate Saussure's linguistic turn. Derrida contended that the Western philosophical tradition privileges spoken (the sonic) over written language (the graphic). It is within this hierarchy that the speaker is presumed to be self-authenticating and in control of meaning. The writer, within this schema, is displaced and, presumably, is not in control of meaning. Saussure, according to Derrida, continues the Western tradition by prioritizing the spoken word over the written word. Derrida describes this as phonocentrism, a suppression of writing. His work seeks to invert the hierarchy and so present writing as a necessary displacement of meaning within language.

Derrida's innovative variations on Saussure's linguistic turn inaugurated postmodernism's sustained dismantling of the metaphysics of presence in the Western philosophical tradition. Derrida's critique of language was followed by critiques of truth and meaning in philosophy. Drawing on the work of the German philosopher Friedrich Nietzsche, Derrida has disrupted the long-held belief that authors intend meaning and that there is a certain truth to be uncovered in texts. Derrida, in the Nietzschean tradition, views philosophy not as a search for truth, but as a rhetorical engagement with the world. Truth and meaning are not fixed: they are metaphorical.

Others have extended Derrida's insights to the study of culture, literature, politics, and psychoanalysis, and, indeed, the displacement of meaning and truth characteristic of post-modernism has proved relevant to diverse academic disciplines. Cast in the best possible light, postmodernism challenges hierarchies and presents a multiplicity of interpretations with an optimism that is not shared by the majority of scholars. Postmodernism's anti-foundationism

is often linked to, if not actually equated with, the logic of late capitalism (Fredric Jameson) and political conservatism. Emphasis on epistemological undecideability and the loss of the subject appears to have persuaded many scholars to view postmodernism as nihilistic and irra-tional. Nevertheless, postmodernism has come to be considered a significant endeavor in culture studies.

The French philosopher Jean-François Lyotard has articulated postmodernism within the aesthetic and political spheres. Lyotard's postmodernism critiques the totalizing tendency of modernity's monolithic world-views. Where there is completion and unity in modernism, one finds deferment and fragmentation in postmodernism. Lyotard's major contribution toward a definition of postmodernism is his theory of *metanarratives* (*grand recits*). Modernity, according to Lyotard, privileges all-encompassing narratives such as fascism, Marxism and capitalism. Lyotard's postmodernism encourages little narratives (*petits recits*) that claim to avoid totalization and preserve heterogeneity. Lyotard's challenge to the tendency to concep-tualize history as events in a linear sequence means that, for him, postmodernism never can be represented in language or in history. Postmodernism for Lyotard is neither a style nor an historical period. Instead, postmodernism is an unrepresentable deferment of conceptualiza-tion and totality.

Given the emphasis that postmodernists place on anti-foundationism and epistemological uncertainty, one can conclude that postmodernism is not easily discernible. It is defined by the use to which it is put within diverse contexts and in the employ of its various exponents. Contemporary Continental philosophy focuses on postmodernism's reassessment of the

Western philosophical tradition, and, in doing so, continually reshapes the contours of the term.

Singularity Unrepeatable linkage of phrases within time and the totality of the universe. Also: the irreducibility of phrases to phrases or events.

Ultimacy The maximal intensity of human desire expressed as the infinite.

NOTES

POSTING

1 Michel Montaigne, *Apology for Raymond Sebond* in *The Complete Works of Montaigne*, trans. D. Frame, Palo Alto: Stanford University Press, 1958, 454–5.
2 Friedrich Nietzsche, *Ecce Homo*, trans. W. Kaufmann, New York: Random House, 1969.
3 Jacques Derrida, *The Margins of Philosophy*, trans. Alan Bass, Chicago: University of Chicago Press, 1982, xvi.
4 Victor E. Taylor and Charles E. Winquist (eds), *Postmodernism: Critical Concepts I–IV*, London and New York: Routledge, 1998, x–xxi.
5 Michel Foucault, *This is not a Pipe*, trans. James Harkness, Berkeley: University of California Press.
6 Jacques Derrida, *Writing and Difference*, trans. Alan Bass, Chicago: University of Chicago Press, 1978, 280.
7 *Ibid.*, 280.
8 *Ibid.*, 281–2.
9 Cf. Jean-François Lyotard, *The Postmodern Condition: A Report on Knowledge*, trans. Geoff Bennington and Brian Massumi, Minneapolis: University of Minnesota Press, 1984.
10 Cf. Jacques Derrida, *Glas*, in which the philosophical and literary threads of a text interweave.
11 Cf. Bill Readings and Bennet Schaber (eds), *Postmodernism Across the Ages: Essays For A Postmodernity That Wasn't Born Yesterday*, Syracuse: Syracuse University Press, 1993.
12 Cf. Barry Smart, *Postmodernity: Key Ideas*, London and New York: Routledge, 1993.
13 Cf. Brian McHale, *Constructing Postmodernism*, London and New York: Routledge, 1992, 19–38.
14 Cf. Jean-François Lyotard, *The Postmodern Explained: Correspondences, 1982–1985*, trans. D. Barry *et al.*, Minneapolis: University of Minnesota Press, 1992, 75–80.

1 PARALOGIES

1 Jean-François Lyotard, *The Differend: Phrases in Dispute*, Minneapolis: University of Minnesota Press, 1988, xiii.
2 Daniel Paul Schreber, *Memoirs of My Nervous Illness*, trans. Ida Macalpine and Richard Hunter, Cambridge, MA: Harvard University Press, 1988, 181.
3 Floyd Merrell, *Pararealities*, West Lafayette: Purdue University Press, 1983, 15–16.
4 Floyd Merrell, *Unthinking Thinking: Jorge Luis Borges, Mathematics, and the New Physics*, West Lafayette: Purdue University Press, 1991, xv.
5 Gilles Deleuze and Felix Guattari, *Kafka: Toward a Minor Literature*, trans. Dana Polan, Minneapolis: University of Minnesota Press, 1986, 7.
6 Jorge Luis Borges, *Ficciones: Obras Completas*, Argentina: Emecé Editores, 1956, 76.
7 Saint Augustine, possibly the first "modernist" (as Eliot was the last), in his *Confessions* (11.15) offers an understanding of the eternality of the sacred: "[T]he only time that can be called present is an instant, if we conceive of such, that cannot be divided even into the most minute fractions, and a point of time as small as this passes so rapidly from the future to the past that its duration is without length. For if its duration were

prolonged, it could be divided into past and future. When it is present it has no duration."

8 T.S. Eliot, "The Waste Land," in *The Norton Anthology of Modern Poetry*, New York: Norton, 1980, 150.

9 Immanuel Kant, *What Is Enlightenment?*, New York: Harper & Row, 1965, 90.

10 Jean-François Lyotard, *The Postmodern Explained*, Minneapolis: University of Minnesota Press, 1994, 15.

11 *Ibid.*, 13.

12 Jean-François Lyotard, *Le Différend*, Paris: Les Éditions de Minuit, 1983, 122.

13 Jean-François Lyotard, *The Postmodern Condition*, 1984, xxiv.

14 *Ibid.*, 61.

2 PARASTRUCTURES OF THE SACRED AND LITERATURE

1 Friedrich Nietzsche, *The Twilight of the Idols*, trans. R.J. Hollingdale, Harmondsworth: Penguin, 1968, 37.

2 Cf. Alan D. Schrift, *Nietzsche's French Legacy: A Genealogy of Poststructuralism*, London: Routledge, 1995.

3 Gilles Deleuze, *The Logic of Sense*, trans. Mark Lester and Charles Stivale, New York: Columbia University Press, 1990, 9.

4 *Ibid.*

5 André Brink, *The Cape of Storms: The First Life of Adamastor*, New York: Simon & Schuster, 1993, 22.

6 The reader enters Brink's novel with a sense of having just walked in on a conversation about the "history of narrative form." The question of what "was" and what "wasn't" actually goes after the missing conversation of early French and Portuguese interpretations of Adamastor.

7 Into hard earth my flesh converted lies
My bones are turned to rocks all rough and, strange,
These members and this form ye see, likewise,
Extended through these spreading waters range;
In fine, my stature of enormous size
Into this Cape remote the Gods did change;
While for redoubled anguish of my woes,
Thetis around me in these waters flows.

(p. 11)

8 Brink, *The Cape of Storms*, 23.

9 William Shakespeare, *The Tempest*, I.ii.344–8.

10 *Ibid.*, I.ii.352–63.

11 Brink, *The Cape of Storms*, 22.

12 Charles H. Long, in "Human Centers: An Essay on Method in the History of Religion," discusses the epistemic crisis of the West as an internal crisis, in so far as epistemology in the West needs a legitimating exterior. He writes:

At what level of the knowing subject did one find a correspondence between what was known and the epistemological center? Cultural evolution might be invoked at this point. The others represent the childhood or adolescence of the human race, a stage familiar to us but long past, since the cultures of the epistemological center are forms of adulthood in this evolutionary metaphorical sense. When some form of the cultural evolutionary structure was not invoked one had recourse to general theories of pathology, fantasy, emotionalism, hysteria, and insanity. In the Western philosophical tradition the metaphysical notion of effective space is translated into the notion of the centeredness of human consciousness. The episteme refers to this centering as a mode of human consciousness. In the form of eidos, arche, ousia, God or Consciousness, the episteme refers us to the constancy of a centered principle from which human thought may have validity. As such it is the basis for thought, truth, and verification. But the epistemic principle constitutes at once a presence and an absence. The paradoxical nature of the epistemic principle consists in the fact that the epistemic principle itself can never be known; it constitutes a presence that allows one to generate data, along the periphery, so to speak, but the actuality of the epistemic principle cannot be known itself. The epistemic principle, the center of homo sapiens, cannot be known itself; it is always transported out of itself into its surrogate, to the data of the periphery.

(p. 407)

3 THE MARGINS OF SUBJECTIVITY AND CULTURE

1 Arthur C. Danto, *Mark Tansey: Visions and Revisions*, New York: Abrams, 1992, 132–5.
2 Naguib Mahfouz, *The Beggar*, New York: Anchor Books, 1990 [1967], 140.
3 *Ibid.*, 99.
4 *Ibid.*, 97–8.
5 T.S. Eliot, *Collected Poems: 1909–1962*, London: Faber & Faber, 1963, 79.
6 Charles E. Winquist, *Desiring Theology*, Chicago: University of Chicago Press, 1995, 9.
7 *Ibid.*, 35
8 *Ibid.*, 14.
9 René Descartes, *Meditations on First Philosophy*, New York: Hackett, 1970, 180.
10 Cf. John Deely, *New Beginnings: Early Modern Philosophy and Postmodern Thought*, Toronto: University of Toronto Press, 1994, esp. Part I.
11 Jacques Derrida, "Plato's Pharmacy," *Dissemination*, trans. Barbara Johnson, Chicago: University of Chicago Press, 1981, 63.
12 *Ibid.*, 64.
13 *Ibid.*, 133.
14 Joseph M. Kitagawa, "The History of Religions in America," in Mircea Eliade and Joseph M. Kitagawa (eds), *The History of Religions: Essays in Methodology*, Chicago: University of Chicago Press, 1959, 3.
15 Phil Patton, "The Great Chicago Fair: A Wonder of Wonders," *Smithsonian* 24(3), 1993, 46.
16 William S. McFeely, *Frederick Douglass*, New York: W.W. Norton & Co., 1991, 368.
17 Cf. *Selected Works of Ida B. Barnett-Wells*, ed. Trudier Harris, New York: Oxford University Press, 1991.
18 William S. McFeely, *Frederick Douglass*, 371.
19 Ida B. Barnett-Wells, *Selected Works*, 54.
20 *Ibid.*
21 M.H. Abrams's remarks are a distillation of his earlier book entitled *Doing Things With Texts* (New York: W.W. Norton & Co, 1989). I have chosen Abrams as a case-study because of his rich opposition to the theories of literary theory. Also, I believe that, more than Ellis and Norris, Abrams has something at stake in his oppositional criticism that is worth addressing.
22 M.H. Abrams, "What Is Humanistic Criticism?," *The Book Press* 3(4), 1993, 14.

23 *Ibid.*, 12.
24 Ray Monk, *Ludwig Wittgenstein: The Duty of Genius*, New York: Free Press, 1990, 536–7.
25 Mark C. Taylor (ed.), *Deconstruction in Context: Literature and Philosophy*, Chicago: University of Chicago Press, 1986, 9.
26 *Ibid.*, 229.
27 Ellis's text can be found in an expanded version in *Against Deconstruction* (Princeton, NJ: Princeton University Press, 1989).
28 John Ellis, "What Does Deconstruction Contribute?", *New Literary History* 19, Winter 1988.
29 Mark C. Taylor (ed.), *Deconstruction in Context*, 234.
30 Henry Staten, *Wittgenstein and Derrida*, Lincoln: University of Nebraska Press, 1986, 98.
31 *Ibid.*, 107.
32 *Ibid.*, 160.

4 DISFIGURING THE SACRED IN ART AND RELIGION

1 André Malraux, *The Voices of Silence*, New York: Doubleday, 1953, 65.
2 *Ibid.*, 65.
3 Mircea Eliade, *Patterns in Comparative Religion*, New York: Meridian Books, 1965, 1.
4 *Ibid.*, 11.
5 *Ibid.*, 12.
6 André Malraux, *The Metamorphosis of the Gods*, New York: Doubleday, 1960, 31.
7 *Ibid.*, 360.
8 Jacques Derrida, *Memoirs of the Blind: The Self-Portrait and Other Ruins*, trans. Pascale-Anne Brault and Michael Nass, Chicago: University of Chicago Press, 1993, 112.
9 Michel Foucault, *The Order of Things: An Archaeology of the Human Sciences*, New York: Vintage, 1973, 4.
10 Foucault cites the passage from Borges with an emphasis on the illogical nature of the categories and the way in which categories contain themselves: This passage (p. xv) quotes a

> certain Chinese encyclopedia [in which it is written that] … "animals are divided into: (a) belonging to the Emperor, (b) embalmed, (c) tame, (d) sucking pigs, (e) sirens, (f) fabulous, (g) stray dogs, (h) included in the present classification, (i) frenzied, (j) innumerable, (k) drawn with a very fine camelhair brush, (l) *et cetera*, (m) having just broken the water pitcher, (n) that from a long way off look like flies."

11 *Ibid.*, 12.
12 David Carroll, *Paraesthetics: Foucault, Lyotard, and Derrida*, New York: Methuen, 1987.
13 *Ibid.*, 56.
14 Mircea Eliade, *Tales of the Sacred and the Supernatural*, Philadelphia: Westminster Press, 1981, 8.
15 *Ibid.*, 9.
16 *Ibid.*, 9.
17 In *Ordeal by Labyrinth: Conversation with Claude-Henri Rocquet* (trans. Derek Coltman, Chicago: University of Chicago Press, 1982, 3, Eliade discusses the various meanings of his name with Rocquet:

> R: Mircea Eliade. That is a beautiful name.
> E: Why do you say that? Eliade: *helios*; and Mircea: *mir*, the Slavic root meaning peace …
> R: … and world?
> E: And world too, yes; or rather, cosmos.
> R: I wasn't thinking primarily of the meaning but of the music.
> E: The name Eliade is Greek in origin

and probably goes back to *helios*. Earlier, it was written Heliade. There were puns on *helios* and *Hellade*: "sun" and "Greek." Only it wasn't my father's real name. My grandfather was called Jeremiah. But in Romania, when someone's a little bit lazy, or very slow or hesitant, people are always quoting the proverb: "Oh, you're like Jeremiah, who couldn't get his cart out." And they used to say it to my father when he was a schoolboy. So he decided that as soon as he came of age he'd change his name. He chose the name Eliade because it had belonged to a very famous nineteenth-century writer: Eliade Radulescu. So he became "Eliade." And I'm grateful to him, because I prefer it to Jeremiah. I like my name.

18 Eliade draws on this experience in his conversation with Claude Henri-Rocquet in *Ordeal by Labyrinth* when he recalls his novel *The Forbidden Forest*. Eliade reconstructs his own experience in his rendering of Stephane's "Sambo" room: "Clearly, in my description of that 'Sambo' room I was calling on my own experience: the extraordinary experience of entering a totally different space" (p. 8).

19 Mircea Eliade, *Autobiography*, Vol. 1: *Journey East, Journey West*, 1988, 23.

20 Joseph M. Kitagawa, *The History of Religions: Understanding Human Experience*, Atlanta: Scholars Press, 1987, 307.

21 Charles H. Long, *Significations: Signs, Symbol, and Images in the Interpretation of Religion*, Philadelphia: Fortress Press, 1986, 24.

22 *Ibid.*, 24.

23 *Ibid.*, 25.

24 Goethe, *Goethe's Botanical Writings*, trans. Mueller Bertha, Honolulu: University of Hawaii Press, 1952, 31.

25 Mircea Eliade, *Patterns in Comparative Religion*, 2.

26 *Ibid.*, 5.

27 *Ibid.*, 7.

28 *bid.*, 7.

29 *Ibid.*, 8.

30 Mircea Eliade, *The Quest: History and Meaning in Religion*, Chicago: University of Chicago Press, 1969, 133.

31 Eliade, *Patterns*, 11.

32 *Ibid.*, 175

33 Mircea Eliade, "History of Religion and a New Humanism" in *History of Religion Journal* 1(1), 1961.

34 *Ibid.*, 2.

35 *Ibid.*, 2.

36 *Ibid.*, 2.

37 *Ibid.*, 7.

38 *Ibid.*, 5.

39 *Ibid.*, 7.

40 *Ibid.*, 8–9.

5 PARA SHOAH

1 In the Foreword to Jean-François Lyotard's *Heidegger and the "Jews"* (Minneapolis: University of Minnesota Press, 1990, ix–x), David Carroll explains the difficulty the survivors' memory has in (re)telling the events of the Holocaust. He points to Shoah as an example of memory which easily can take multiple political, moral, and military paths. The difficulty, as Carroll's reading of Lyotard suggests, is in understanding the Holocaust as a foundation for political or ethical action:

> The literature of the concentration camps indicates that most survivors of the Shoah, who are hostage to the impossible obligation and task of talking/not talking about "that," are more modest than this. They know

that if it is impossible to tell of what happened, this is why they must tell and retell what happened. This gives them no privilege; on the contrary they find themselves in an impossible narratological, political, and moral situation each time they begin to talk about "that." If they do not know what to tell or how to tell, they do know that it will do no "good" to tell, that what will be ignored or misunderstood, perhaps even used for dogmatic political, religious, and moral purposes that most often probably make it seem as if it would have been better not to have told at all. But because they have to tell, they do, but never easily and most often with a feeling that they have betrayed something or someone by doing, so that their telling has betrayed what it has told and those who cannot tell.

2   James E. Young, *Holocaust Memorials and Meaning: The Textual of Memory*, New Haven: Yale University Press, 1993, 7.

3   Sophocles, *Œdipus the King*, New York: Harper & Row, 1960, 34.

4   Plato, *Republic*, trans. G.M.E. Grube, New York: Hackett, 1992, ll.620e–621d.

5   Cf. Yosef Hayim Yerushalmi, *Zakhor: Jewish History and Jewish Memory*, Seattle: University of Washington Press, 1982, 5.

6   Plato, *Phaedrus*, Princeton, NJ: University of Princeton Press, 1980, III.249c.

7   Mircea Eliade, *Myth and Reality,* New York: Meridian Books, 1970, 119.

8   *Ibid.*, 121.

9   Gilles Deleuze and Felix Guattari, *What Is Philosophy?*, New York: Columbia University Press, 1994, 15–16.

10   Mark C. Taylor, *Nots*, Chicago: University of Chicago Press, 1993, 1.

11   In *Dialogues* (New York: Columbia University Press, 1987, 124), Deleuze writes his way to a more accessible articulation of singularity through the example of lines:

> Whether we are individuals or groups, we are made up of lines and these lines are very varied in nature. The first kind of line which forms us is segmentary – of rigid segmentarity (or rather there are many lines of this sort): family–profession; job–holiday; holiday–family–and then school–and then the army–and then the factory–and then retirement. And each time, from one segment to the next, they speak to us saying: "Now you're not a baby any more"; and at school, "You're not at home now"; and in the army, "You're not at school now".… In short, all kinds of clearly defined segments, in all kinds of directions, which cuts us up in all senses, packets of segmentarized lines. At the same time, we have lines of segmentarity which are more supple, as it were molecular. It's not that they are more intimate or personal – they run through societies and groups as much as individuals. They trace out little modifications, they make detours, they sketch out rises and falls: but they are no less precise for all this, they even direct irreversible processes. But rather than molar lines with segments, they are molecular fluxes with thresholds and quanta. A threshold is crossed, which does not necessarily coincide with a segment of more visible lines.

These second lines are the linchpin for Deleuzean "politics" in that these second lines open on to other possibilities or becomings. In other words, the fluidity of the second lines "compensate" the rigidity of the first lines by continually positing the phrase "... it could be otherwise."

12 Jean François Lyotard, "The Sign of History," in *The Lyotard Reader*, trans. Goeff Bennington, Oxford: Blackwell University Press, 1989, 400.

13 *Ibid.*, 363.

14 Gilles Deleuze, *Dialogues*, viii.

15 F. Scott Fitzgerald, "Crack-up," in Arthur Mizener (ed.), *The Fitzgerald Reader*. New York: Scribners, 1963, 405.

16 In *A Thousand Plateaus* (p. 206), Deleuze and Guattari cite Fitzgerald's description of his relationship with Zelda:

> Perhaps fifty percent of our friends and relations will tell you in good faith that it was my drinking that drove Zelda mad, and the other half would assure you that it was her madness that drove me to drink. Neither of these judgements means much of anything. These two groups of friends and relations would be unanimous in saying that each of us would have been much better off without the other. The irony is that we have never been more in love with each other in all our lives. She loves the alcohol on my lips. I cherish her most extravagant hallucinations. ... In the end, nothing really had much importance. We destroyed ourselves. But in all honesty, I never thought we destroyed each other.

17 *Ibid.*, 206–7.

18 Gilles Deleuze, *The Logic of Sense*, 102.

19 *Ibid.*, 100.

20 *Ibid.*, 104.

21 Ludwig Wittgenstein, *Philosophical Investigations*, in Mark C. Taylor (ed.), *Deconstruction in Context*, Chicago: University of Chicago Press, 1986, 228.

22 Deleuze, *The Logic of Sense,* 178.

23 Immanuel Kant, *The Critique of Pure Reason*, New York: St Martin's Press, 1959, 383–4.

24 In *The Differend* (pp. 22–3), Lyotard states:

> The differend is the unstable state and instant in which something which ought to be able to be phrased cannot yet be phrased. This state involves silence which is a negative sentence, but it also appeals to sentences possible in principle. What is ordinarily called sentiment signals this fact. "You can't find the words to say it," and so on. A great deal of searching is necessary to find new rules of formation and linkages of sentences capable of expressing the differend betrayed by sentiment, if one does not wish this differend to be immediately stifled as litigation, and the alert given by sentiment to have been useless. It is the stake of a literature, a philosophy, perhaps of a politics, to bear witness to differends by finding idioms for them.
>
> In the differend, something "asks" to be phrased, and suffers the wrong of not being able to be phrased. So humans who thought they used language as an instrument of communication learn by this feeling of pain which accompanies silence (and of pleasure which accompanies the invention of a new idiom) that they are the object of language's demand, not that they increase to their own benefit the quantity of information which can be communicated in existing idioms, but that they recognize that what is to be phrased exceeds what they can phrase at the moment, and that they must allow the institution of idioms which do not yet exist.

25 *Ibid.*, 22.

128

26 Lyotard, *The Lyotard Reader*, 363–4.

27 The concept of witness is a complicated one for anyone reading Lyotard. In *The Differend*, he uses the word "witness" to call attention to the impossibility of such a person. In *The Postmodern Condition*, on the other hand, Lyotard calls upon the reader to bear witness to the differend and mulitiplicity.

28 Lyotard, *The Lyotard Reader*, 364.

29 Lyotard, *The Differend*, 101.

30 Lyotard, *The Lyotard Reader*, 363.

31 In "Result" (*The Differend*, 152), Lyotard discusses the result as the end of the Hegelian dialectic. He qoutes Adorno in order to set the rules for linking: "A chain of phrases comes to be linked together on the basis of this rule. Here are some of its links: 'It lies in the definition of the negative dialectic that it will not come to rest in itself, as if it were total. This is a form of hope.'" Lyotard's discussion in *The Differend* often turns to the Hegelian dialectic in order to further complicate the event of Auschwitz. To invest in the dialectic is to end Auschwitz, and it is this moment of closure on which Lyotard wages war.

32 Jean François Lyotard and Jean-Loup Thebaud, *Just Gaming*, Minneapolis: University of Minnesota Press, 1985, 60.

33 I am acutely aware of dangers or possible connotations of "game" here. I think Lyotard has to be given some room in the sense that "game" has been a word used to describe the actions of language around a set of rules (e.g. by Wittgenstein).

34 Lyotard and Thebaud, *Just Gaming*, 60.

35 Leon Uris's novels *Exodus* and *The Haj,* for example, illustrate this ethics out of the Holocaust by constructing a narrative in which the Holocaust is the ontological truth of the state of Israel. This is an injustice in the Lyotardian sense because the voices of those who cannot speak are spoken for in the articulation of a politics.

36 Lyotard, *The Lyotard Reader*, 362.

37 Jacques Derrida, *The Margins of Philosophy*, Chicago: University of Chicago Press, 1981, xvii.

38 *Ibid.*

6 PARASACRED GROUND(ING)S

1 Jean Baudrillard, *Symbolic Exchange and Death*, trans. Ian Hamilton Grant. London: Sage Publications, 1993, 126.

2 *Ibid.*, 127.

3 Jacques Derrida, *Aporias*, trans. Thomas Dutoit. Stanford: Stanford University Press, 1993, 6.

4 Sophocles, *Œdipus at Colonus*, New York: Harper & Row, 1974, 88.

5 *Ibid*, 92

6 Jean-François Lyotard, "Critical Reflections," *Artforum* 29(8), 1991, 92.

7 PARAGRAVE

1 Søren Kierkegaard, *Concluding Unscientific Postscript*, trans. D.F. Swenson and W. Lowrie, Princeton, NJ: Princeton University Press, 1968, 213.

2 D.H. Lawrence, *The Man Who Died*, New York: Vintage, 1953, 211.

8 EPILOGUE

1 Søren Kierkegaard, *The Diary of Søren Kierkegaard*, ed. Peter Rohde, New York: Citadel Press, 1993, 25–6.

GLOSSARY

1   Peter A. Angeles writes
    (*HarperCollins Dictionary of
    Philosophy*,1992, 65):

> Definition (from Latin, *definire*,
> limit, end, be concerned with
> boundaries of something). 1. the
> meaning of a word (either its
> ordinary, commonly accepted
> meaning, or the meaning stipulated
> [intended] by the user. 2. the
> description of the essential
> characteristics (properties, attributes,
> qualities, features) of a thing or idea.
> The principal function of a definition
> is to present meanings for terms that
> are not clearly understood in a
> context of other terms (and their
> meanings) that *are* clearly
> understood. Definitions increase
> vocabulary and impart information.
> They attempt to prevent ambiguity,
> obscurity, unintelligibility,
> imprecision, vagueness, and
> complexity (by, for example, making
> it possible to substitute single words
> for sometimes cumbersome
> meanings) . Definitions are, in a
> general sense, stipulative. They are
> resolutions – declared intentions as
> to (a) how to use words in a certain
> manner, and (b) how they are used.

2   *Ibid.*, 65.

BIBLIOGRAPHY

Adorno, Theodor, *Negative Dialectics*, New York: Continuum, 1966.

Althusser, Louis, "Cremonini, Painter of the Abstract," in *Lenin and Philosophy*, New York: Monthly Review, 1971.

Altizer, Thomas J.J., *Mircea Eliade and the Dialectic of the Sacred*, New York: Greenwood, 1975.

Angeles, Peter A. (ed.), *The HarperCollins Dictionary of Philosophy*, 2nd edn, New York: Harperperennial, 1992.

Barthes, Roland, *Mythologies*, trans. Annette Lavers, London: Jonathan Cape, 1972.

Bataille, Georges, *Visions of Excess: Selected Writings, 1927–39*, Minneapolis: University of Minnesota Press, 1985.

Baudrillard, Jean, *Simulations*, trans. Paul Foss, Paul Patton and Philip Beitchman, New York: Autonomedia, 1983.

—— *Symbolic Exchange and Death*, trans. Ian Hamilton Grant, London: Sage Publications, 1993.

Borges, Jorge-Luis, *Labyrinths*, New York: New Directions Publishing, 1964.

—— *Personal Anthology*, New York: Grove Weidenfield, 1967.

Brink, André, *The Cape of Storms: The First Life of Adamastor*, New York: Simon & Schuster, 1993.

Buci-Glucksmann, Christine, *Baroque Reason: The Aesthetics of Modernity*, trans. Patrick Camiller, Thousand Oaks: Sage Publications, 1994.

Burgin, Victor, *The End of Art Theory*, Atlantic Highlands: Humanities Press International, 1988.

Carroll, David, *Paraesthetics: Foucault, Lyotard and Derrida*, New York: Methuen, 1987.

Critchley, Simon, *The Ethics of Deconstruction: Derrida and Levinas*, Oxford: Blackwell, 1992.

Danto, Arthur C., *Mark Tansey: Visions and Revisions*, New York: Abrams, 1992.

Deleuze, Gilles, *Kant's Critical Philosophy: The Doctrine of Faculties*, trans. Hugh Tomlinson and Barbara Habberjam, Minneapolis: University of Minnesota Press, 1983.

—— *The Logic of Sense*, trans. Mark Lester and Charles Stivale, New York: Columbia University Press, 1990.

—— *The Fold*, Minneapolis: University of Minnesota Press, 1993

—— *Essays Critical and Clinical*, trans. Daniel W. Smith and Michael Greco, Minneapolis: University of Minnesota Press, 1997.

Deleuze, Gilles and Guattari, Felix, *Anti-Oedipus: Capitalism and Schizophrenia*, trans. Robert Hurley, Minneapolis: University of Minnesota Press, 1983.

—— *A Thousand Plateaus: Capitalism and Schizophrenia*, Minneapolis: University of Minnesota Press, 1988.

—— *What Is Philosophy?*, New York: Columbia University Press, 1994.

Derrida, Jaques, *Writing and Difference*, trans. Alan Bass, London: Routledge, 1978.

—— *Dissemination*, trans. Barabara Johnson, Chicago: University of Chicago Press, 1981.

—— *Spurs – Nietzsche's Styles*, trans. Barbara Hanlon, Chicago: University of Chicago Press, 1981.

—— *The Margins of Philosophy*, trans. Alan Bass, Chicago: University of Chicago Press, 1982.

—— *The Truth in Painting*, trans. Geoff Bennington and Ian MacLeod, Chicago: University of Chicago Press, 1987.

—— *Glas*, trans. Richard Rand and John P. Leavey, Lincoln: University of Nebraska Press, 1990.

—— *Acts of Literature*, ed. Derek Attridge, London: Routledge, 1992.

—— *Aporias*, trans. Thomas Dutoit,

Stanford: Stanford University Press, 1993.

—— *Memoirs of the Blind: The Self-Portrait and Other Ruins*, trans. Pascale-Anne Brault and Michael Nass, Chicago: University of Chicago Press, 1993.

—— *The Gift of Death*, trans. David Willis, Chicago: University of Chicago Press, 1996.

Dilthey, Wilhelm, *Hermeneutics and the Study of History*, ed. Rudolph A. Makkreel and Frithjof Rodi, Princeton Princeton University Press, 1996.

Eliade, Mircea, "History of Religion and a New Humanism," *History of Religion Journal* 1(1), 1961.

—— *Patterns in Comparative Religion*, New York: Meridian Books, 1965.

—— *The Quest: History and Meaning in Religion*, Chicago: University of Chicago Press, 1969.

—— *Ordeal by Labyrinth*, Chicago: University of Chicago Press, 1980.

—— *Autobiography*, Vol. 1: *Journey East, Journey West, 1907–1937*, trans. Mac Linscott Ricketts, San Francisco: Harper & Row, 1981.

—— *Tales of the Sacred and the Supernatural*, Philadelphia: The Westminster Press, 1981.

—— *Autobiography*, Vol. 2: *Exile's Odyssey, 1937–1960*, trans. Mac Linscott Ricketts, Chicago: University of Chicago Press, 1988.

Eliot, T.S., *Selected Essays*, London: Faber & Faber, 1986.

Foucault, Michel, *The Order of Things: An Archaeology of the Human Sciences*, New York: Vintage, 1973.

—— *Power/Knowledge: Selected Interviews and Other Writings, 1972–1974*, New York: Pantheon Books, 1981.

—— *This is not a Pipe*, trans. James Harkness, Berkeley: University of California Press, 1982.

Freud, Sigmund, *Collected Papers*, Vol. IV,

trans. Joan Riviere, New York: Basic Books, 1959.

Gasché, Rodolphe, *The Tain of the Mirror*, Cambridge: Harvard University Press, 1986.

Goethe, Johann Wolfgang von, *Goethe's Botanical Writings*, trans. Bertha Mueller, Honolulu: University of Hawaii Press, 1952.

Hardt, Michael, *Gilles Deleuze: An Apprenticeship in Philosophy*, Minneapolis: University of Minnesota Press, 1993.

Heidegger, Martin, *Poetry, Language, Thought*, trans. Albert Hofstadter, New York: Harper & Row, 1971.

Jabès, Edmond, *The Book of Questions*, Middleton: Wesleyan University Press, 1972.

Jencks, Charles, *What Is Postmodernism?*, New York: Academy Editions/St Martin's Press, 1987.

Kafka, Franz, *The Trial*, New York: Penguin, 1965.

Kairys, David, *The Politics of Law: A Progressive Critique*, New York: Pantheon, 1982.

Kant, Immanuel, *The Critique of Pure Reason*, New York: St Martin's Press, 1959.

—— *The Critique of Judgement*, Oxford: Clarendon Press, 1980.

Kitagawa, Joseph M., *The History of Religions: Understanding Human Experience.* Atlanta: Scholars Press, 1987.

Klein, Richard, *Cigarettes Are Sublime*, Durham: Duke University Press, 1994.

Krauss, Rosalind, *The Originality of the Avant-Garde and Other Modernist Myths*, Cambridge, MA: MIT Press, 1985.

Krieger, Murray, *The Institution of Theory*, Baltimore: Johns Hopkins University Press, 1994.

Kroker, Arthur and Cook, David, *The Postmodern Scene*, New York: St Martin's Press, 1986.

Lacan, Jacques, *The Four Fundamental Concepts of Psycho-Analysis*, ed. J.A. Miller, trans. A. Sheridan, New York: Norton, 1981.

Levi, Primo, "The Drowned and the Saved," in *Survival in Auschwitz*, New York: Collier Books, 1976.

Lévi-Strauss, Claude, *Structural Anthropology*, trans. Claire Jacobson and Brooke G. Schoepf, New York: Basic Books, 1963.

Long, Charles H., "Human Centers: An Essay on Method in the History of Religion," *Soundings* 61(3), 1978.

—— *Significations: Signs, Symbols, and Images in the Interpretation of Religion*, Philadelphia: Fortress Press, 1986.

Lyotard, Jean-François, "The Dream-work Does Not Think," trans. Mary Lydon, *Oxford Literary Review* 6(1), 1983.

—— *Driftworks*, New York: Semiotext(e), 1984.

—— *The Postmodern Condition: A Report on Knowledge*, trans. Geoff Bennington, Minneapolis: University of Minnesota Press, 1984.

—— *The Differend: Phrases in Dispute*, Minneapolis: University of Minnesota Press, 1988.

—— *Peregrinations: Law, Form, Event*, New York: Columbia University Press, 1988.

—— "Discussions, or Phrasing 'After Auschwitz'," in Andrew Benjamin (ed.), *The Lyotard Reader*, Oxford: Blackwell, 1989.

—— "Judiciousness in Dispute, or Kant after Marx," in Andrew Benjamin (ed.), *The Lyotard Reader*, Oxford: Blackwell, 1989.

—— *Duchamp's TRANS/formers*, Venice: Lapis Press, 1990.

—— *Heidegger and "the Jews,"* trans. Andreas Michel and Mark Roberts, Minneapolis: University of Minnesota Press,1990.

—— "Critical Reflections," *Artforum,* 29(8), 1991.

Lyotard, Jean François and Jean-Loup Thebaud, *Just Gaming*, trans. Wlad Godzich, Minneapolis: University of Minnesota Press, 1985.

Mahfouz, Naguib, *The Beggar*, New York: Anchor Books, 1990 [1967].

Malraux, André, *The Voices of Silence*, New York: Doubleday, 1953.

—— *The Metamorphosis of the Gods*, New York: Doubleday, 1960.

Merkel, Jayne, "Art On Trial," *Art in America* 78(12), 1990.

Merrell, Floyd, *Pararealities: The Nature of Our Fictions and How We Know Them*, West Lafayette: Purdue University Press, 1983.

Miller, Donald L., "The White City," *American Heritage* 44(4), 1993.

Monk, Ray, *Ludwig Wittgenstein: The Duty of Genius*, New York: Free Press, 1990.

Norris, Christopher, *The Truth about Postmodernism*, Oxford: Blackwell, 1993.

Plato, *Phaedrus*, in Edith Hamilton (ed.), *Plato: The Collected Dialogues*, Princeton: Princeton University Press, 1980.

—— *Republic*, trans. G.M.A. Grube, New York: Hackett Publishing, 1992.

Rabelais, François, *Gargantua and Pantagruel*, trans. Sir Thomas Urquhart and Peter Motteux, Chicago: Encyclopedia Brittanica, 1952.

Readings, Bill, *Introducing Lyotard: Art and Politics*, New York: Routledge, 1991.

—— "The End of the Political," in *Jean François Lyotard: Political Writings*, trans. Bill Readings and Paul Geiman, Minneapolis: University of Minnesota Press, 1993.

Shakespeare, William, *The Tragedy of Hamlet, Prince of Denmark*, The Riverside Shakespeare edn, Boston: Houghton Mifflin Company, 1974.

—— *The Tragedy of King Lear*, The Riverside Shakespeare edn, Boston: Houghton Mifflin Company, 1974.

—— *The Merchant of Venice*, The

Riverside Shakespeare edn, Boston: Houghton Mifflin Company, 1974.

—— *The Tempest*, The Riverside Shakespeare edn, Boston: Houghton Mifflin Company, 1974.

Smart, Barry, *Postmodernity: Key Ideas*, London and New York: Routledge, 1993.

Taylor, Mark C., *Deconstructing Theology*, New York: Crossroad Publishing, 1982.

—— "Introduction: System ... Structure ... Difference ... Other," *Deconstruction in Context: Literature and Philosophy*, ed. Mark C. Taylor, Chicago: University of Chicago Press, 1986.

—— *Altarity*, Chicago: University of Chicago Press, 1987.

—— *Erring: A Postmodern A/Theology*, Chicago: University of Chicago Press, 1987.

—— "Nothing Ending Nothing," in *Theology at the End of the Century*, ed. Robert Scharlemann, Charlottesville: University of Virginia Press, 1990.

—— *Tears*, Albany: SUNY Press, 1991.

—— *Disfiguring: Art, Architecture, Religion*, Chicago: University of Chicago Press, 1992.

—— *Nots*, Chicago: University of Chicago Press, 1993.

Taylor, Mark C. and Saarinen, Esa, *Imagologies: Media Philosophy*, London: Routledge, 1994.

Teraoka, Masami "Portrait of Robert Mapplethorpe," *Artforum International*, 29(3), 1990.

Unger, Roberto Mangageira, *The Critical Legal Studies Movement*, Cambridge: Harvard University Press, 1986.

Winquist, Charles *The Transcendental Imagination: An Essay in Philosophical Theology*, The Hague: Martinus Nijhoff, 1972.

—— *Epiphanies of Darkness: Deconstruction in Theology*, Philadelphia: Fortress Press, 1986.

—— "The Silence of the Real: Theology at the End of the Twentieth Century," in Robert Scharlemann (ed.), *Theology at the End of the Century*, Charlottsville: University of Virginia Press, 1990.

—— *Desiring Theology*, Chicago: University of Chicago Press, 1995.

Wittgenstein, Ludwig, *Philosophical Investigations*, in Mark C. Taylor (ed.), *Deconstruction in Context*, Chicago: University of Chicago Press, 1986.

Yarbrough, Stephen R., *Deliberate Criticism: Toward a Postmodern Humanism*, Athens: University of Georgia Press, 1992.

INDEX